Trinidad & Tobago

Sarah Cameron

Credits

Footprint credits
Editor: Stephanie Rebello
Production and layout: Emma Bryers
Maps: Kevin Feeney

Publisher: Patrick Dawson
Managing Editor: Felicity Laughton
Advertising: Elizabeth Taylor
Sales and marketing: Kirsty Holmes

Photography credits
Front cover: Mikeledray/
Dreamstime.com
Back cover: Superstock/Wolfgang
Kaehler/age fotostock

Printed in India by Thomson Press Ltd,
Faridabad, Haryana

Every effort has been made to ensure
that the facts in this guidebook are
accurate. However, travellers should
still obtain advice from consulates,
airlines, etc, about travel and visa
requirements before travelling. The
authors and publishers cannot accept
responsibility for any loss, injury or
inconvenience however caused.

The content of Footprint *Focus Trinidad
& Tobago* is based on Footprint's
Caribbean Islands Handbook, which
was researched and written by
Sarah Cameron.

Publishing information
Footprint *Focus Trinidad & Tobago*
1st edition
© Footprint Handbooks Ltd
September 2014

ISBN: 978 1 909268 35 7
CIP DATA: A catalogue record
for this book is available from
the British Library

® Footprint Handbooks and the
Footprint mark are a registered
trademark of Footprint Handbooks Ltd

Published by Footprint
6 Riverside Court
Lower Bristol Road
Bath BA2 3DZ, UK
T +44 (0)1225 469141
F +44 (0)1225 469461
footprinttravelguides.com

Distributed in the USA by
National Book Network, Inc.

Contents

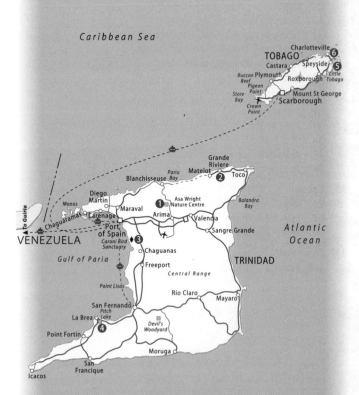

Caribbean Sea

TOBAGO
Charlotteville ⑥
Castara Speyside
Plymouth Roxborough ⑤
Buccoo Pigeon Point *Little Tobago*
Reef
Store Mount St George
Bay Scarborough
Crown Point

Grande
Riviere
Paria Matelot
Bay ② Toco
Blanchisseuse
Balandra
Diego *Bay*
Martin Asa Wright
Monos Maraval Nature Centre ①
Chaguaramas Carenage Arima Valencia
Port
VENEZUELA of Spain Sangre Grande
To Guiria Caroni Bird ③ *Atlantic*
Sanctuary Chaguanas *Ocean*
Gulf of Paria Freeport
Central Range **TRINIDAD**
Point Lisas
Río Claro
San Fernando Mayaro
Pitch
La Brea *Lake*
④ *Devil's*
Woodyard
Point Fortin
Moruga
San
Francique
Icacos

Columbus Channel

N
20 km
20 miles

4 ● Trinidad & Tobago

The most southerly of the Caribbean arc of islands, Trinidad and Tobago are only just off the coast of Venezuela, yet they share little of the culture of South America. The people now living on the islands have come from far-flung homelands and are a cosmopolitan mix of African, East Indian, Chinese, European and Syrian. This means that on these islands you can listen to calypso, parang or chutney soca, while eating East Indian, Chinese or West Indian dishes. In Trinidad, the food and music are so good that the island's influence has spread not only through the Caribbean but worldwide.

Trinidad's ebullient carnival is world famous and attracts thousands of visitors ready and willing to spend days 'jumping up' and parading in the hot sun, carried along by the crowd. Fuelled by rum and street food, all and sundry don brilliantly gaudy costumes and, in a riot of colour, join in the dancing and singing to the latest calypsos.

However, wealth comes from oil, gas and manufacturing rather than tourism and many of its beaches remain empty of foreign tourists and fairly unspoilt. Beach tourism has been developed on the smaller, sister island of Tobago, where hotels are spreading around the coastline, but there are still glorious bays and coves and resorts are small and low key.

These forested islands are brimming with flora and fauna, and birdwatching is a major attraction. The species found here are directly related to those found in South America, as well as in the Caribbean islands. The forests and wetlands are denser and contain a greater diversity of animal and plant life than anywhere else in the Caribbean. There are several protected areas and wildlife sanctuaries where, in addition to the birds, you can find mammals such as monkeys and manatee, as well as reptiles such as iguanas and cayman.

Planning your trip

Best time to visit Trinidad and Tobago

As with everywhere in the Caribbean the climate is tropical and temperatures reach a maximum of 30°-31°C year round. Trinidad and Tobago are hilly, forested islands and attract plenty of rain to keep them lush and green. The driest time of year is usually January-April, coinciding with the winter peak in tourism as snow birds escape to the sun. Temperatures then can fall to 20°C during the day, depending on altitude, but are normally in the high 20°s, tempered by cooling trade winds and the occasional shower. The mean annual temperature is about 26°C. At other times of the year greater humidity can make it feel hotter if you are away from the coast, where the northeast trade winds are a cooling influence. Rain tends to fall in the afternoon and not for very long. Trinidad and Tobago are far enough south to escape the worst of the hurricane season which afflicts most of the Caribbean in June-November. However, tropical storms can cause flooding and mudslides. The wettest months are June-August, followed by September-November.

The main event of the year is Carnival, attended by thousands of revellers. With pre-Carnival events in January leading up to the pre-Lenten Carnival in February, this is one of the best in the world, full of spontaneity and not to be missed. There are also year-round festivals, many of which have Indian origins, such as the Hindu festival of Phagwa, or Holi, in February/March and Divali in October/November. Muslim festivals are also celebrated, such as Eid-ul-Fitr, marking the end of Ramadan. See Festivals in Trinidad and Tobago, page 17.

Getting to Trinidad and Tobago

Air
There are two international airports, **Piarco International** on Trinidad and ANR **Robinson International** at Crown Point on Tobago.

Flights from the UK British Airways (www.britishairways.com) and **Caribbean Airlines** (www.caribbean-airlines.com) fly from London to Trinidad. **British Airways**, **Virgin Atlantic** (www.virgin-atlantic.com) and **Monarch** (www. monarch.co.uk) fly to Tobago.

Flights from the rest of Europe Condor (www.condor.com, part of the **Thomas Cook** group) flies from Frankfurt to Tobago but there are no flights in to Trinidad.

Flights from North America Airlines fly to Trinidad from Miami and New York on a daily basis, with less frequent flights from Orlando and Fort Lauderdale. **Jet Blue** (www.jetblue.com) also flies from New York and Fort Lauderdale. **American Airlines** (www.americanairlines.com) flies from Miami, while **United Airlines** (www.united.com) flies from Houston, both with connecting services from other US cities. **West Jet** (www.westjet.com) and **Caribbean Airlines** fly to Trinidad from Toronto.

Flights from the Caribbean Trinidad is a hub for both **Caribbean Airlines** and LIAT (www.liatairline.com), connecting Trinidad and Tobago with other islands, including Antigua, Bahamas, Barbados, Curaçao, Grenada, Jamaica, St Lucia, St Vincent, Sint Maarten and the mainland Guyana, Suriname and Venezuela. **Conviasa** (www.conviasa.aero) also connects Venezuela with Trinidad.

Airport information On Trinidad, **Piarco International Airport**, www.tnt airports.com/piarco, is 16 miles southeast of Port of Spain. The enormous terminal has plenty of space, if few comfortable places to sit. Downstairs, the departure area has ATMs, several fast food restaurants (quiet one upstairs) and a **First Citizens Bank** foreign exchange office near the Customs exit open 0600-2200, shops selling snacks, crafts and souvenirs. Extensive duty free is available on the way in to Trinidad as well as on departure. There are a number of duty-free shops; upstairs for a fairly well-stocked bookshop, a bar and (very expensive) fast food. In the duty-free area on the left side of the staircase there is the **Millennium Finance – Cambio** for foreign exchange transactions. Outside the Customs exit there is a tourist information desk run by the **Tourism Development Company** (TDC).

Try to avoid overnight connections here. Airline schedules ensure that it is possible to arrive at Piarco after the check-in counters have closed until next morning, so you cannot go through to the departure lounge. There is a 24-hour **left luggage** service near the Customs exit, TT$8 per hour per item, TT$15 per day. If you are in transit always check that your bags have not been off-loaded at Piarco, some are not checked through despite assurances.

On Tobago, **ANR Robinson International Airport** at Crown Point is within walking distance of the hotels in the southwest. It is also uncomfortable for a long wait, often with no food available after you have been through immigration control. There are a few shops, snack bars and a bank with an ATM outside the terminal building but only a small duty-free inside. If you are booked on a large aircraft, such as **Virgin Atlantic**'s, expect long, slow queues from check-in, past the departure tax booth, all the way up the stairs to the X-ray machines, which can take an hour to clear.

Sea

You can get to Trinidad and Tobago from the north by cruise ship or by private yacht, but there is currently no international passenger service to other islands. There is a ferry service between Güiria, Venezuela, and **Pier One**, at Chaguaramas, (see www.pier1tt.com, T6344472 ext 25 in Trinidad or T(58) 2-949-821556, Miguel Acosta, in Venezuela). Originating in Trinidad, the ferry departs **Pier One** on Wednesdays at 0830 (check in 0630), arriving around 1200, returning from Güiria at 1530, arriving 1930, fares US$115 one way, US$230 return, US$138 day trip, plus departure tax of US$13 from Trinidad and US$23 from Venezuela. Check what documents you need for Venezuela.

Yachts Chaguaramas (Trinidad) and Scarborough (Tobago) are the ports of entry. In Chaguaramas, take the boat to the customs dock (T6344341, open 24 hours) to clear on arrival in Trinidad and fill in combined customs and immigration form. Overtime fee for after hours, 1600-0800, weekends and holidays, so it pays to arrive during normal working hours. A clearance out certificate from your last port is required. Immigration and Customs at Scarborough is open 0800-1600 weekdays, T6390006.

Departure by sea Clear out with customs and immigration. Pay port fees for each month that the boat was in Trinidad and Tobago waters. To go from one island to the other clear out with Immigration and in on the new island. Clear customs only when making final departure. New arrivals must be signed aboard the vessel as crew by immigration in Chaguaramas.

Departure by air Boats can be left in storage; yacht yards will help with paperwork, present it to customs and clear with immigration within 24 hours of departure for exemption from departure tax. When returning to Trinidad by air, go to third party line at airport to get paperwork to take with baggage to Chaguaramas customs to clear. Arriving outside office hours leave boat parts for weekday review. Arriving guests should have return ticket and letter to Trinidad immigration stating vessel name and official number.

Information *The Boca* is a useful monthly 'yachtie' magazine available locally or at www.boatersenterprise.com. The annual *Boaters Directory* (produced December, T6342622) lists services for yachties: free to arriving yachties. The **Yacht Services Association** ⓘ *T6344938, www.ysatt.org*, is also extremely helpful.

Marinas The Trinidad marinas are all west of Port of Spain along the coast to Chaguaramas. **Trinidad and Tobago Yacht Club (TTYC)** ⓘ *Western Main Road, T6337420*, a private club, leases members' slips to visiting yachts when available, 60 in-water berths, security, restaurant, bar, laundry. **Trinidad and Tobago Sailing Association (TTSA)** ⓘ *Chaguaramas, T6344519, www.ttsailing. org*, a private members' association with moorings and anchorage available to visiting yachts, full service haul-out yard, 15-ton marine hoist, moorings, repair shed, bar, restaurant, laundry. **Power Boats Mutual Facilities** ⓘ *Chaguaramas, T6344303, www.powerboats.co.tt,* haul-out and storage, 50-ton marine hoist, 23 in-water berths, boat storage, marine supplies, fibreglass repairs, welding, woodworking, apartments, grocery, restaurant, laundry. **Peake Yacht Services** ⓘ *Chaguaramas, T6344420, www.peakeyachts.com*, full service marina, 150-ton marine hoist, capable of beams to 31 ft, 21 in-water berths, boat storage, 10-room hotel, restaurant, wi-fi, laundry, skilled maintenance. **IMS Yacht Services** ⓘ *Chaguaramas, T6252104, www.imsyacht.com*, full service haul-out and storage yard, 70-ton marine hoist, paint shop, chandlery, sailmaker, fibreglass repair, welding, woodworking, sandblasting, restaurant, laundry. **Crews Inn Yachting Centre** ⓘ *Chaguaramas, T6344384, www.crewsinn.com*, is best equipped with on-shore facilities, including a hotel with pool and gym, restaurant, ATM, **Econocar** car rental agency, T6342154, hair salon, duty-free liquor store. Tardieu Marine nearby will lift and dry storage. **Sweet Water Marina**, also nearby at ⓘ *2 Stella Maris Dr, Western Main Road, T6344046, www.sweetwatermarinatt.com*, has a restaurant. All locations charge a fee to anchored boats for use of shoreside facilities.

Transport in Trinidad and Tobago

Air

Caribbean Airlines, www.caribbean-airlines.com, flies the Trinidad to Tobago route offering 24, 25-minute, daily flights, US$24 one way, US$48 return, children under 12 half price. Tickets can be bought online or at the airport counter. Departures, however, are often heavily booked at weekends and holidays, particularly Christmas and afterwards, also pre- and post-Carnival and Easter weekend (at other times tickets can sometimes be bought the same day).

Boat

Taking the ferry between Trinidad and Tobago is time-consuming; it is easier to fly. The Port Authority of Trinidad and Tobago (PATT) operates two fast ferries, the T&T Express and the T&T Spirit which take about 2½ hours, US$16 return ticket (TT$50 one way, children 3-12 half price). *The Warrior Spirit*, a Ro-Ro vessel designed to take cargo, is older and less comfortable, taking about 8-10 hours, US$12 (TT$37.50 economy class one way, TT$80 cabin class). For the schedule, see https://ttitferry.com. Tickets are not available online, but are sold at authorized travel agents or the **Port Authority** ① *T6392417 in Tobago or T6254906 in Trinidad, www.patnt.com) on the docks, office hours in Port of Spain are Mon-Fri 0730-1600.* At peak times such as Christmas, Carnival and Easter it is best to book several weeks ahead. Weekends also get booked up quickly. You need a boarding pass and not just a ticket before you can board. The ferry takes cars but it is easier to rent separately each end.

A **Water Taxi** service runs between Port of Spain and San Fernando to relieve pressure on the congested roads and this is much the easiest way to travel between the two cities. There are six 45-minute crossings a day Monday-Friday (mostly in the mornings for commuters from San Fernando and in the afternoons for the return journey from Port of Spain), one on Saturday, closed Sunday, and the crossing is fast and comfortable, US$2.40 (TT$15) one way. There is also a 15-minute ferry from Port of Spain to Chaguaramas Monday-Friday 0730, return 1615; Saturday 1030, return 1600 (allowing connection with the 1645 crossing from Port of Spain to San Fernando), US$1.60 (TT$10) one way, docking at La Soufriere Maritime Ltd on Western Main Road. Tickets can be bought at the Water Taxi terminals at Flatrock, Lady Hailes Avenue, San Fernando and the Cruise Ship Complex, Port of Spain. For more information contact the **Chaguaramas Development Authority (CDA)** ① *T6344227*, or **National Infrastructure Development Company Limited (NIDCO)** ① *T6245137 (Port of Spain Office)* and *T6529980 (San Fernando Office), http://nidco.co.tt.* Shuttle buses run Monday-Friday from the terminal in Port of Spain to the east of the city, west of the city and Queen's Park Savannah, US$0.45. Buses also run from La Soufriere in Chaguaramas east to Tembladora (The Boardwalk), north to

Macqueripe and west to Tetron. Passengers can hop on and off these buses all day until their return sailing. The CDA also runs a tour bus with daily tours of the peninsula as well as dropping off passengers for tours to the Gasparee Caves.

Road

Driving is on the left and the roads are narrow and winding. There is no left turn allowed on a red light and U-turns are also illegal. It is mandatory for the driver and all passengers to wear seatbelts in the front and back seats and children under 12 must have specially fitted seats.

On **Trinidad** there are dual carriageways from Port of Spain south to San Fernando, west to Diego Martin and east to Arima, but these and other roads are not of a high standard. Neither is the driving. No-entry signs are misleadingly placed; some have a little notice underneath saying they apply only to public transport (private cars can enter). The rush hour on Trinidad starts early and ends late. Traffic is very heavy. Allow at least an hour to leave Port of Spain in the late afternoon. There may be traffic jams at surprising times, for example returning from Chaguaramas in the small hours of weekends, or after the beach on Sunday afternoon; or whenever there is a police roadblock exercise. There are pot holes almost everywhere and traffic weaves about all over the place at high speed to avoid them. Taxis (licence plates beginning with H) tend to stop suddenly in the middle of the road to pick up/drop off passengers. Allow a full day if going from Port of Spain to Toco in the northeast or to the far southwest, if you want to have time to see anything or relax before returning. On rural roads there are prominent kilometre posts. The older mile posts are still often there too and are used in some postal addresses (eg 21 mile post, Toco Road). In some of the more chaotic suburbs, light poles have a similar role (eg M Smith, opposite Light Pole 12, Smith Trace, Morvant).

On **Tobago** the roads are fairly good in the south but storms and landslides frequently disrupt passage in the north. Mountain bikes are fine if you can stand the hills and the heat.

Landslides are a risk on both islands during (or after) heavy rain, and can block roads, for example along the north coast of Trinidad. Flooding may also block roads particularly in the Caroni plains of central Trinidad.

Hitchhiking is not advised.

Bus Buses are run by the state-owned **Public Transport Service Corporation** (PTSC). On Trinidad, the remodelled South Quay railway station, called City Gate, is the main terminal for both buses and maxi taxis. You can get information showing how to reach the various sights by bus. On all routes, purchase your ticket at the kiosk before boarding the bus; you may have to tender the exact fare. On Tobago all buses originate from the bus terminal in Scarborough. Schedules are changed or cancelled frequently.

The word 'taxi' includes most forms of public transport, encompassing buses, taxis, route taxis (*colectivos*) and maxi taxis (minibuses and vans). The word 'travelling' means going by public transport rather than by private car. **Route taxis** work on the same basis as a bus, picking up passengers on a fixed route, except that they are a car. They are very cheap but not as comfortable as an ordinary taxi (see below) and it can be hard to distinguish between them, so ask the driver. Like buses, they have marked stands, although you can hail them and be dropped anywhere along the route. They often toot their horn if they have a vacant seat. If you want to go off the fixed route you pay extra. The route taxi system is difficult for the foreigner, being based on everyone knowing every car and therefore where it is going, but official route taxis have an 'H' (for hire) at the start of the licence plate. Ask for directions for where to assemble for a particular route. During rush hour they often pass full, however, and in general it takes time to master the system. They are the only means of transport on some suburban routes, such as to St Ann's, and in rural areas away from main roads. Travelling to remote areas may involve three or more taxis, which is not really a problem; just ask where the next one stops. Major routes run all night and are amazingly frequent during the day, others become infrequent or stop late at night. Route taxis are the most common method of public transport on Tobago. Route taxis and maxi taxis depart from Lower Scarborough for western destinations, and from Main Street (Windward Road) in Scarborough for other destinations. **Maxi taxis**, also following fixed routes, are privately owned and come in two sizes, seating 12 or 24 people. Maxi taxis are frequent and go as fast as the traffic will allow, often a bit faster.

There are some safety issues to be considered when taking route and maxi taxis. See pages 81 and 114 for more information on routes.

Car hire Some car hire companies only rent for a minimum of three days. Rental can be difficult on Trinidad, particularly at weekends and around Carnival, because of heavy demand. It is best to make reservations in advance. Small, older cars can be rented from US$35 a day upwards, unlimited mileage, check the tyres before driving off. Most cars, including rental vehicles, are right-hand drive. The wearing of seat belts by the driver and front seat passenger is mandatory. The use of mobile phones is illegal while driving, except in 'hands-free' mode. The penalty for talking or texting while driving is US$240 or three months' imprisonment. **National Petroleum** (NP) is the most common gas/petrol station, charging a little under US$1 per litre for premium unleaded fuel. While there are plenty of NP stations on main roads in urban areas, they are infrequent in rural areas.

International and most foreign driving licences are accepted for up to 90 days; after that you need to apply for a Trinidad and Tobago licence and take a written test. All drivers must always carry their licence and insurance with them. Documents are inspected at police road blocks, which are frequent on many main roads. Do not leave anything in your car, theft is frequent. Be careful where you park in Port of Spain, police 'wreckers' are diligent and will tow the car away. You will then need to pay to retrieve it and you need to show your driver's licence and insurance documents.

See pages 81 and 114 for a list of car hire companies.

Taxi Look for cars with first letter 'H' on licence plates (no other markings). Taxis are expensive. On Trinidad, taxis operate from the main hotels, and from Independence Square. Helpful drivers approach all stray white people on Independence Square, but this can be confusing if you are really looking for a route taxi (or a beer). There are fixed fares (eg US$30 to the airport from central Port of Spain during the day, US$45 after 2200), but agree on a price before the journey and determine whether the price is in TT dollars or US dollars. On Tobago it costs only US$6 for the short journey from the airport to the Coco Reef Hotel, but US$65 for the journey from the airport all the way to Charlotteville. All fares rise by 50% after 2200. Drivers expect a tip of about 10%. Book ahead if you have a flight to catch. **Phone A Taxi**, T6288294, and **Kalloo's**, T6229073, slightly cheaper day or night. Take a taxi if you have a complicated journey, or you have heavy baggage, or it is raining. At night it can be a lot cheaper than getting robbed. A taxi tour can be negotiated for about US$25 per hour, depending on how many people are in the car. A simple city tour of Port of Spain is US$60 for one person, US$35 per person for two people and US$25 per person for three or more passengers. An island tour costs US$250/130/90 per person respectively. Contact St Christopher Taxicab Co-operative, T6387322, or at the big hotels.

There are also 'pirate' or 'PH' taxis with the P registration of a private car, which cost the same as the ordinary route taxis. Use these with caution; they are unlicensed and not insured for carrying paying passengers. Robberies have been reported. 'Ghost' taxis accept fares and drive off with your luggage as well – be warned.

Where to stay in Trinidad and Tobago

There are many hotels on the islands including some very good guesthouses and smaller hotels. The islands are notable for having a large number of independent, privately owned hotels, with very few international chains represented. The **Hilton**, **Hyatt** and the **Radisson** in Port of Spain are the exceptions rather than the rule and exist mainly to capture the business market. Information about accommodation can be obtained from **TDC**, see Tourist information, page 28. All properties listed have met minimum

Price codes

Where to stay

$$$$ over US$150 $$$ US$66-150
$$ US$30-65 $ under US$30

Price codes refer to a standard double/twin room in high season.

Restaurants

$$$ over US$12 $$ US$7-12 $ under US$7

Price codes refer to the cost of a two-course meal, excluding drinks or service charge.

national standards and are enrolled in the **Trinidad and Tobago Tourism Industry Certification** (TTTIC) programme. However, many of the independent hotels in Port of Spain and elsewhere have been criticized for poor service, lack of maintenance and being in need of renovation. Hotel tax (11%) and service (10%) is charged by all hotels, usually as a single charge of 21.5%. If you intend to stay in Trinidad for Carnival you must book a hotel well in advance. Most hotels raise their prices steeply and some insist you stay for the full period. If arriving without accommodation arranged at Carnival time, the tourist office at the airport may help to find you a room in a hotel, or with a local family, though both options will be expensive. Reservations are sometimes cancelled and hotels which have not sold their full package may make rooms available at the last minute. For most of the year, hotels in Port of Spain cater almost exclusively for business visitors and rooms can be hard to find if your visit coincides with a conference. *Discover Trinidad and Tobago* has a full listing of the smaller bed and breakfast places to stay.

Camping Camping is unsafe and not recommended except on organized tours or on private land with security.

Food and drink in Trinidad and Tobago

Food

Trinidad and Tobago offer some of the best food in the Caribbean, with a wide variety of influences from around the world coming together to make a distinctive fusion cuisine. The culinary history is accredited to the islands being occupied by the Spanish, French and British, who in turn used the labour of the Amerindians, Africans, Chinese and East Indians, supplemented later by immigrants from the Middle East and Portugal. The variety of one-pot stews, hearty dishes relying on meat and carbohydrates, comes from the traditions of African slaves. Curries were brought from India, with emphasis on vegetables and pulses. Many of the very sweet desserts and snacks can be traced to Indian roots. Southern Trinidad is considered the home of Indian cooking, although it is found everywhere. The ubiquitous Chinese restaurant is on nearly every street, with chefs adapting their repertoire according to local ingredients. Pork with dasheen is one example and local spices and herbs give the food a distinctive flavour.

The climate and the fertile soil contribute to the wealth of fresh ingredients available, while the waters around the islands teem with delicious seafood. In particular, crab and shrimp are excellent. There is a local fish called salmon, which is a white fish, no relation to the Scottish/Canadian variety. Smoked herring and salt cod are often eaten with a fried bake, especially for breakfast. The many tropical fruits and vegetables grown locally include: large and juicy pineapples, pawpaws, very good sapodillas, and starchy eddoes and yam tanias. Varieties of bananas include the mini sweet siquier, the large plantain (eaten fried) and the savoury green fig (a banana, not a fig). Citrus season is January to March. Fruit and vegetables to seek out later in the year include mangoes (a huge variety: julie, graham, peter, starch, pineapple, long, doudou, etc) and large, creamy avocados (locally called *zaboca*). Coconut water from a fresh nut is refreshing, usually sold around the Savannah, Port of Spain and on Independence Square after dark. A distinctive local herb is *chadon beni*, which tastes a bit like coriander.

The *roti*, a chapatti pancake which comes in various forms, filled with peppery stew, shrimp or vegetable curries, is very good and cheap. *Buss up shut* is a torn-up *paratha*, or Indian bread accompaniment to curries. Creole food (African-influenced, home-cooked food) is popular at lunchtime. *Pelau*, savoury peas and rice and meat cooked with coconut and pepper, is also good. Some other popular meat dishes are cow-heel soup and chicken-foot and pig-foot souse. Use the local pepper sauce in moderation unless you are accustomed to chilli dishes. Non-meat eaters are well catered for. Try *saheena*, deep-fried patties of spinach, dasheen, split peas and mango sauce. *Pholouri* are fritters made with split peas. *Buljol* is a salt fish with onions, tomatoes, avocado and pepper. *Callaloo* is a thick soup based on dasheen leaves. *Doubles* are curried chickpeas (*channa*) in two pieces of fried *barra* (mini pancakes), eaten for breakfast and bought from street stalls across the country. A *hops* is a crusty bread roll. If you go to Maracas Bay, have shark-and-bake, a spicy fried bread sandwich of fried shark with a variety of sauces such as tamarind, garlic, *chadon beni*; kingfish-and-bake and shrimp-and-bake are alternatives. Sugar cakes, made with grated coconut, are also good. *Pastelles/pastilles*, eaten at Christmas, are maize flour parcels stuffed with minced meat, olives, capers and raisins, steamed in a banana leaf. Dumplings are a must on Tobago, and are particularly good with crab. A local sweet in Tobago is benny balls, made from sesame seeds. Salt prunes (Chinese) and red mango are on sale almost everywhere. There's a huge variety at the lookout before you get to Maracas.

Drink
A local non-alcoholic drink is *mauby*, slightly bitter and made from the bark of a tree. Sorrel is a bright red Christmas drink made from sepals of a plant from the hibiscus family. There is also ginger beer, and you can get sorrel and ginger beer shandy. Fresh lime juice is recommended; it is sometimes served with a dash of Angostura bitters. There are lots of very fine Angostura rums (www.angostura.com) to try, many of which are better without punch or Coke and savoured on the rocks. Local beers are **Carib** and **Stag**, both owned by the same company, which also brews **Carlsberg**, **Mackeson**, **Royal Stout** and **Guinness**; **Samba**, a Pilsner-type lager beer is a locally brewed independent. From the same company is **Stud Power Stout**, which contains several herbs considered aphrodisiacs.

Eating out
Hotels and guesthouses serve a wide variety of European, American and traditional West Indian (or Creole) dishes, including pork souse, black pudding, roast suckling pig, *sancoche* and *callaloo* stews, and many others. There is also a strong East Indian influence and lots of Chinese restaurants too. If you've a yen for the best pepper shrimps in the Caribbean, the Chinese restaurants in Trinidad are generally good, with chefs often direct from China. There is plenty of choice, and the menus are fairly 'authentic', even in some cheap places, although others can be greasy and nasty. There are many gourmet restaurants taking Trini food to exalted heights, but often the best food is found on the street. Look for the vendors with the longest queues and you won't be disappointed. In Port of Spain, the area for the best nightlife and street food is St James in the west, where night owls can always find vendors selling barbecue and jerk meats, roti, ice cream, Creole corn soup, *ital* (vegetarian) food and drinks of many varieties. Queen's Park Savannah is another good place to try local snacks, from coconut water and coconut jelly to oysters, served in a glass with a dash of lime and a spicy sauce. Tobago's best restaurants are generally small and family-owned; seafood is good and crab is a speciality. They are dotted around the island, often in scenic locations so you can enjoy a pleasant lunch overlooking a bay or beach, or sip a sunset cocktail on a veranda before dinner. Scarborough is not well-endowed with restaurants, but it is improving with the arrival of Spanish tapas and Italian pizza places.

Opening hours are liable to change at short notice. Many places close on Sunday, and some public holidays. They may close or reduce their hours over

Carnival when most customers are too preoccupied to eat properly and staff are otherwise engaged. Most of the smarter restaurants do lunch for around US$20 but are much more expensive in the evening. A free magazine, *Cré Olé*, www.créolé.com, prints menu extracts and prices for better-known places, useful for pre-dinner browsing.

Festivals in Trinidad and Tobago

There is a festival or special event of some kind just about every week of the year in Trinidad. Make sure you use enough sunblock. See www.gotrinidad andtobago.com for a full list of events.

Jan New Year's Day.

Feb/Mar The **Hindu festival of Phagwa**, or **Holi**, the colour, or spring, festival on the day of the full moon in the month of **Phagun** (Feb/Mar). Usually celebrated at Tunapuna Hindu School and the Divali Nagar. Everyone gets squirted with brightly coloured dyes (*abeer*); strict Hindus have their doubts about some of the dancing styles.

Feb/Mar Carnival Mon and Tue before Ash Wed (not officially holidays). The best carnival parades and music in the Caribbean, managing to be both well-rehearsed and spontaneous. Great fun, see box, page 20.

30 Mar **Spiritual Baptist (Shouter) Liberation Day**. A public holiday since 1996, it celebrates the right of Spiritual Baptists to worship. The original Baptists in Trinidad were African Americans, former slaves who fought for Britain in the War of American Independence, later settling in Princes Town, Laventille and Caroni district. They were banned from practicing their religion in 1917-1951.

Mar/Apr **Good Fri** and **Easter Mon** are public holidays and the long weekend is one of the most popular for a trip to the beach. The annual **National Kite Flying Championship** is held at Queen's Park Savannah, Port of Spain, on Easter Sun. **Buccoo Goat and Crab Races** are held at the Buccoo Integrated Facility on Tobago on **Easter Tue**.

Apr The **Tobago Jazz Experience**, www.tobagojazzexperience.com, attracts many international celebrities as well as local and regional performers, with concerts at a variety of venues around the island and associated cultural events such as walks, tours, goat racing and lots of opportunities to sample local food.

Late Apr/early May **Point Fortin Borough Week**, with steel bands and street parties.

May **La Divina Pastora**, in the southern town of Siparia, celebrated by Catholics and Hindus.

30 May **Indian Arrival Day**, celebrating the arrival of Indian indentured labourers in 1845 when

Music

Calypsonians (or kaisonians, as the more historically minded call them) are the commentators, champions and sometime conscience of the people. This unique musical form, a mixture of African, French and, eventually, British, Spanish and East Indian influences, dates back to Trinidad's first 'shantwell', Gros Jean, late in the 18th century. Since then it has evolved into a popular, potent force, with both men and women (also children, of late) battling for the Calypso Monarch's crown.

This fierce competition takes place at the Sunday night Dimanche Gras show, which in turn immediately precedes the official start of J'Ouvert at 0400 on the Monday morning, marking the beginning of Carnival proper. Calypsonians band together to perform in 'tents' (performing halls) in the weeks leading up to the competition and are judged in semi-finals, which hones down the list to six final contenders. The season's songs blast from radio stations and sound systems all over the islands and visitors should ask locals to interpret the sometimes witty and often scurrilous lyrics, for they are a fascinating introduction to the state of the nation.

Currently, party soca tunes dominate, although some of the commentary calypsonians, like Sugar Aloes, are still heard on the radio. There is also a new breed of 'Rapso' artists, fusing calypso and rap music. Chutney, an Indian version of calypso, is also popular, especially since the advent of radio stations devoted only to Indian music. Chutney is also being fused with soca, to create 'chutney soca'.

Pan music has a shorter history, developing this century from the tamboo-bamboo bands which

225 Indians arrived to work on the sugar plantations to take the place of African slaves after eventual emancipation. The day was declared a public holiday in 1996.

19 Jun Labour Day. Corpus Christi (determined by the Christian calendar) falls 2 Thu after Pentecost. Roman Catholic churches organize processions. It coincides with the start of the rainy season and many farmers plant their pigeon peas and corn in the hope that their crops will be plentiful.

Jul St Peter's Day in Carenage and fishing villages along the north coast is the first weekend in Jul. The **Tobago Heritage Festival** lasts for the second fortnight of the month, with historical re-enactments, variety shows in communities around the island, parades, more goat and crab racing and lots of different local foods to try.

1 Aug Emancipation Day. First celebrated in 1985, it marks the freeing of the slaves on this day in 1983. There are lots of historical and cultural activities involving the African diaspora.

made creative use of tins, dustbins and pans plus lengths of bamboo for percussion instruments. By the end of the Second World War (during which Carnival was banned) some ingenious souls discovered that huge oil drums could be converted into expressive instruments, their top surfaces tuned to all ranges and depths (the ping pong, or soprano pan, embraces 28 to 32 notes, including both the diatonic and chromatic scales). Aside from the varied pans, steel bands also include a rhythm section dominated by the steel, or iron men. For Carnival, the steel bands compete in the grand Panorama, playing calypsoes which are also voted on for the Road March of the Year. Biennally, the **World Steel Band Festival** highlights the versatility of this music, for each of the major bands must play a work by a classical composer as well as a calypso of their choice. On alternate years the National Schools Steel Band Festival is held, in late October/early November. A pan jazz festival is held annually in November, with solos, ensembles and orchestras all emphasizing the versatility of the steel drum, www.pantrinbago.co.tt.

Other musical forms in this music-mad nation include parang (pre-Christmas). Part of the islands' Spanish heritage, parang is sung in Spanish and accompanied by guitar, cuatro, mandolin and tambourine. The big annual **parang** competitions are at Paramin, in a natural hillside amphitheatre, and at Lopinot. For the Hindu and Muslim festivals, there are East Indian drumming and vocal styles such as chowtal, which is particularly associated with Phagwa in early March.

29 Aug Feast of St Rose of Lima is celebrated in Arima. Descendants of the original Amerindians come from all over the island to walk in solemn procession round the church.
31 Aug Independence Day. To mark the anniversary of independence from Britain in 1962 there are military and police parades at the Queen's Park Savannah, followed by a steel band and 'jump up' through the streets of St James.
Sep Tobago Fest is Tobago's carnival equivalent. There are masquerade bands from Trinidad, a night 'mas', steel band competitions, calypso shows and street parties.
24 Sep Republic Day.
25-26 Dec Christmas Day, Boxing Day. Although this is a Christian festival, it is celebrated by most of the population, with people decorating their houses and eating traditional foods such as black cake and pastilles, and drinks such as sorrel and ginger beer. Date depends on the Hindu religious calendar but is usually **Oct/Nov** The Hindu festival of lights, **Divali**,

Carnival and the visual arts

The most exciting introduction to the culture of this republic is the **Carnival**, or 'De Mas', as locals refer to the annual 'celebration of the senses'. Alongside a strong oral/literary tradition goes a highly developed visual culture, reflecting the islands' racial mix. The most obvious examples are the designs for the carnival bands, which often draw on craft skills like wire bending, copper beating and the use of fibreglass moulds.

Carnival is a national obsession. It is an extraordinary spectacle and a vibrant time to be in Trinidad. Much of the country's artistic energy is poured into these heady few days. Carnival in Trinidad is considered by many to be safer, more welcoming to visitors and artistically more stimulating than its nearest rival in Rio de Janeiro. Commercialization is undermining many of the greatest Mas' traditions, but some of the historical characters such as the **Midnight Robber** and the **Moko Jumbies** can be glimpsed at the Viey La Cou old-time Carnival street theatre at Queen's Hall a week before Carnival and often at **J'Ouvert** (pronounced joo-vay) on Carnival Monday morning, and in small, independent bands of players. But it's a great party, enlivened by hundreds of thousands of costumed masqueraders and the homegrown music, calypso and steel band (usually referred to as 'pan').

A few islanders are world-famous for their creative output. A fabled, controversial Mas' designer is Peter Minshall, who designed the opening ceremony for the 1992 Barcelona Olympic Games and for the Atlanta Games in 1996. Michel Jean Cazabon, born 1813, was the first great local artist (an illustrated biography by Geoffrey MacLean is out of print, but there is an illustrated book on the Lord Harris Collection with plenty of information). Contemporary work to look out for includes paintings and other artwork by Christopher Cozier, Irenée Shaw, Sarah Beckett, Che Lovelace, Mario Lewis, Wendy Nanan, Emheyo Bahabba (Embah), Francisco Cabral, and Anna Serrao and Johnny Stollmeyer. Other established artists include Pat Bishop, Isaiah Boodhoo, LeRoy Clarke, Kenwyn Crichlow and Boscoe Holder.

celebrates the birth of Lakshmi, the goddess of light and symbolizes the triumph of light over darkness. It is a family affair and involves a lot of good food in Indian homes, with pretty oil lamps or *deyas* burning outside, lighting the way home for the mythic hero, Ram, returning after a long quest. The display at Felicity in central Trinidad is spectacular, but go early to avoid the traffic.

The **Hosay**, or **Hosein Festival**, commemorating the killing of Mohammed's grandsons, Hussein

Folklore in Tobago

Tobago's culture is far more rooted in African traditions than Trinidad's, which is more of a cosmopolitan mix. Many of these can be seen at the **Tobago Heritage Festival** in the second half of July (http://tobagoheritagefestival.com), which was created to preserve the island's cultural traditions, whether in language, music, dance or food. Tobagonians like to compare their Heritage Festival with Trinidad's carnival in importance to the people, although they celebrate carnival as well. Where Trinidad has calypso, Tobago has speech bands when costumed characters declaim their speeches in rhyme. Drumming is frequently seen on Tobago, but look out for tambrin music which is driven by three shallow goatskin tambrin drums (high-pitched cutter, roller and boom bass), together with a fiddle and steel triangle. Tambrin music accompanies traditional dances such as the 'reel and jig', the 'heel and toe' and 'brush back'.

At the Heritage Festival, try and catch the **Ole Time Wedding**, a tradition celebrated since Independence in 1962 at the Moravian Church in Moriah (TT$50 per person). There is a huge cast of characters mimicking the grand marriages of the white plantocracy of the 19th century. While you wait (interminably) for the bride to arrive, the 'village macco' regales the congregation with gossip about her, using the 'ole' talk. The groom and his companions dress in tailcoats and white trousers, they carry umbrellas and top off their outfits with enormous stovepipe hats, while all the ladies are decked out in colourful Victoriana with wonderful hats. There are many characters symbolizing different aspects of 'ole time' life: one woman carries a trunk on her head representing the bride's trousseau and the couple's journey through life, another supports a breadfruit for the bride's virginity, a coal pot and iron on another's head are the tools the bride needs for her married state. Rice is thrown over the couple to bring fertility. After the church ceremony there is a procession by the wedding party to the reception following music trucks. They perform the 'brush back' dance, which is three steps back, dip and three steps forward, reflecting the ups and downs of life.

and Hassan in battle, starts 10 days after the first appearance of the new moon in the Moharrun month of the Moslem calendar (10-11 days earlier each year). These are Shia festivals, commemorating martyrdom. Most Trinidad Muslims are Sunni. There are night-time processions accompanied by drumming, symbolic of war drums. St James is the best area to see them in Port of Spain, but Hosay processions are also held in Curepe, Tunapuna, Couva and Cedros. Although beer and rum are on sale nearby, try not

Books

Some authors to investigate are CLR James, Samuel Selvon, Shiva Naipaul, all now deceased, as well as Shiva's more famous brother, VS Naipaul, who in 2001 won the Nobel Prize for Literature. His novels include *A Bend in the River*, *A House for Mr Biswas*, *Miguel Street* and *Half a Life*, but he has also written travel books and semi-autobiographical fiction spanning Asia, Africa and the Caribbean with tightly drawn characters and insightful commentary on displaced peoples and fractured societies, with great sensitivity and often much humour. Another Nobel winner, the St Lucian Derek Walcott, spent many years with the Trinidad Theatre Workshop. Also, look out for works by the historian and past prime minister Dr Eric Williams, Earl Lovelace and Valerie Belgrave (whose *Ti Marie* has

been described as the 'Caribbean *Gone with the Wind*'). Although the tradition of performance poetry is not as strong here as in, say, Jamaica (calypso fulfils some of its role), the monologues of Paul Keens-Douglas are richly entertaining and a great introduction to the local dialect or patois (if now somewhat dated).

There is a good local publisher, MEP (www.meppublishers.com), founded in 1991 by journalist Jeremy Taylor and Joanne Mendes. As well as *Caribbean Beat* and *Discover Trinidad and Tobago* magazines, they publish a string of informative books including *Views from the Ridge*, *Flowers of Trinidad & Tobago*, *Orchids of Trinidad & Tobago* and *A Naturalist's Notes: the Biological Diversity of Trinidad & Tobago*, all by Julian Kenny; *Halcyon Days: Sculpture 1987-91*, *Bolero* and

to flaunt it immediately around the *tajjas/tadjahs*, the elaborately decorated models of mosques. Also celebrated is the Muslim festival of **Eid ul-Fitr**, marking the end of Ramadan and the start of the Muslim New

Year (changes according to religious calendar, with the date announced about 2 weeks ahead). It is a time for gatherings of family and friends with feasting, including many sweet treats such as sawine, a sweet vermicelli.

Resurrection to Dance all by Luise Kimme; *Letters from London* by CLR James; *A Naturalist's Year* by Richard ffrench; *The Elusive Eric Williams* by Ken Bhoodoo and *Birds of Trinidad and Tobago: a Photographic Atlas* by Russel Barrow.

The best birdwatching books are *A Guide to the Birds of Trinidad & Tobago* by Richard ffrench (foreword by Carol J James), illustrated by John P O'Neill (Comstock Publishing Associates, third edition, 2013), the classic book on the islands' bird life now updated with more and better illustrations; *Helm Field Guides' Birds of Trinidad & Tobago* by Martyn Kenefick, Robin L Restall and Floyd E Hayes, now in its second edition, 2011; *Birds of Trinidad and Tobago* by Richard ffrench (author) and Roger Neckles (photographer) (Macmillan Caribbean Natural History, 2004); and *A Birdwatchers' Guide to Trinidad & Tobago*, by William L Murphy (Prion Birdwatchers' Guide Series, 2004). Depending on your level of knowledge and interest, you may want a combination of a couple of these guides.

Hikers and nature lovers should try to get hold of *The Trinidad & Tobago Field Naturalists' Club Trail Guide*, edited by PL Comeau, IR Potter and PK Roberts, now in its second edition, 2006 (www.ttfnc.org), which covers a number of trails together with information on geology and the environment as well as offering advice when planning a hike. There is also the slightly outdated (1992) *Nature Trails of Trinidad* by ffrench and Bacon, edited by Victor Quesnel, in the second edition.

Essentials A-Z

Accident and emergency

Police T999; **fire** and **ambulance** T990. To report a crime T555, toll-free. **Coast guard** T6344440 or VHF 16, www.ttdf.mil.tt/ttcg.

Clothing

Beachwear is for the beach. In the evening people dress more smartly but are not formal. Light cotton clothing is best for the tropical weather but pack a sweater, cardigan or wrap for cool evenings. Do not wear military or camouflage clothing; it is illegal in Trinidad and Tobago. Anyone dressed in camouflage risks being detained by Customs officials and having the garments confiscated.

Customs and duty free

Duty-free imports: 200 cigarettes or 50 cigars or 250 g tobacco, 1.5 litres wine or spirits, and TT$3000 worth of gifts, see www.customs.gov.tt. Passengers in transit, or on short visits, can deposit goods such as liquor with customs at the airport and retrieve it later free of charge. Duty-free prices at the airport are low. Duty-free shops are accessible to arriving passengers.

Drugs

Do not be tempted to dabble in narcotics. Penalties are severe and foreigners and their vehicles may be searched. Tourists have occasionally been killed as a result of suspected drug deals and many more are behind bars after failed attempts to take narcotics home.

Electricity

110 or 220 volts, 60 cycles AC.

Embassies and consulates

For a list of embassies and consulates in Trinidad and Tobago, see http://embassy.goabroad.com.

Health

There are both public and private hospitals. The public health care system is free to residents and non-residents.

See your GP or travel clinic at least 6 weeks before departure for general advice on travel risks and vaccinations. Try phoning a specialist travel clinic if your own doctor is unfamiliar with health in the region. Make sure you have sufficient medical travel insurance, get a dental check, know your own blood group and, if you suffer a long-term condition such as diabetes or epilepsy, obtain a **Medic Alert** bracelet (www.medicalert.org.uk).

The major risks posed in the region are those caused by insect disease carriers such as mosquitoes and sandflies. The key parasitic and viral diseases are dengue fever, malaria and chikungunya (also known as chik V). The occurrence of **malaria** is reported as very low in Trinidad and Tobago and advice is to investigate fever promptly, rather than take prophylaxis. **Dengue fever** is particularly hard to protect against as the mosquitoes can bite throughout the day as well as night (unlike those that carry malaria); try to wear clothes that cover arms and legs and also use effective mosquito repellent. Mosquito nets dipped in permethrin provide a good physical and chemical barrier at night. Trinidad is currently considered to be hyperendemic for dengue fever, meaning there is sustained circulation of the virus in the population at relatively high incidence levels. There is also evidence of more than one subtype in circulation. **Chikungunya** virus is relatively new in the Caribbean. It does not kill, unlike dengue, but causes severe joint pain which can last for a year or two after infection. **Yellow fever**, which is also spread through mosquito bites, has been found in monkeys in southern and southeastern Trinidad and inoculation would be sensible if you are planning to travel in rural areas. Yellow fever has not been found on Tobago.

Some form of **diarrhoea** or intestinal upset is almost inevitable, the standard advice is always to wash your hands before eating and to be careful with drinking water and ice. In a restaurant buy bottled water or ask where the water has come from. Food can also pose a problem; be wary of salads if you don't know whether they have been washed or not. Inoculation against **Hepatitis A** (and **Hepatitis B**) is recommended.

There is a constant threat of **tuberculosis (TB)** and although the BCG vaccine is available, it is still not guaranteed protection. It is best to avoid unpasteurized dairy products and try not to let people cough and splutter all over you.

Websites

www.cdc.gov Centres for Disease Control and Prevention (USA). **www.nhs.uk/nhsengland/ Healthcareabroad/pages/ Healthcareabroad.aspx** Department of Health advice for travellers. **www.fitfortravel.scot.nhs.uk** Fit for Travel (UK), a site from Scotland providing a quick A-Z of vaccine and travel health advice requirements for each country. **www.itg.be** Prince Leopold Institute for Tropical Medicine. **www.nathnac.org** National Travel Health Network and Centre (NaTHNaC). **www.who.int** World Health Organisation.

Insurance

Take out some form of travel and health insurance, wherever you're travelling from and to. This should cover you for theft or loss of possessions and money, the cost of medical and dental treatment, cancellation of flights, delays in travel arrangements, accidents, missed departures, lost baggage, lost passport and personal liability and legal expenses. Also check on the inclusion of 'dangerous activities', such as climbing, diving, horse riding, even trekking, if you plan to do any.

There are many insurance companies and policies to choose from, so it's best to shop around. Reputable student travel organizations often offer good-value policies. Note that some companies will not cover those over 65 and you may need specialist services.

Language

English is the official language, although you may also find Spanish, Chinese, Hindi, German, French or a French patois spoken.

LGBT (lesbian, gay, bisexual and transgendered)

Male to male and female to female sexual relationships are illegal in Trinidad and Tobago and punishable by prison sentences of 10 years or more. For more information, see http://ilga.org.

Maps

Large-scale and island-wide maps of both islands can be bought from the **Lands and Survey Division**, 118 Frederick St, T6279204, Mon-Fri 0800-1600. Some areas are out of print.

Money → US$1 = TT$6.35; UK£1 = TT$10.85; €1 = TT$8.60 (Jul 2014)

Currency
The currency is the Trinidad and Tobago dollar, TT$. Notes are for

TT$1, 5, 10, 20 and 100. Coins are for 1, 5, 10, 25 and (rarely) 50 cents. The Trinidad and Tobago dollar was floated in 1993, but the float is tightly managed and the exchange rate has remained around TT$6.25 = US$1 since 1996. US dollars are widely accepted by businesses at a rate of about TT$6=US$1, but sterling and euro are less welcome. Banks generally change only certain currencies: Eastern Caribbean, US, Barbados and Canadian dollars, euro, sterling and Swiss franc. On departure you can change TT$ back into US$ at the bank at Piarco (open until 2200). It is difficult to exchange TT$ on other islands (but quite easy in Guyana).

Plastic/ATMs/banks
Credit cards are accepted almost everywhere on Trinidad. On Tobago there are no banks outside Scarborough (except at ANR Robinson Airport); traveller's cheques are changed by large hotels but if you are travelling to the northern end of the island make sure you have enough TT$ as not everyone accepts US$. ATMs are widely distributed and accept credit and debit cards. **RBTT (Royal Bank of Trinidad and Tobago)** ATMs in West Mall, Park St, Maraval, Gulf City, La Romaine and the airport will give US$ as well as TT$.

Currency cards
If you don't want to carry lots of cash, pre-paid currency cards allow you to preload money from your bank account, fixed at the day's exchange rate. They look like a credit or debit

card and are issued by specialist money changing companies, such as **Travelex** and **Caxton FX**. You can top up and check your balance by phone, online and sometimes by text.

Cost of living/travelling

You can save money on food by eating from stalls on the street, where a meal can cost US$3 or less. In a restaurant meals cost between US$10-100, while if you are self-catering, allow about US$50 a week for 2 people eating fresh fruit and vegetables in season and some meat and fish. Car hire will cost anything from US$50 a day, while excursions or day trips range from US$50-100 per person. The cheapest accommodation is in bed and breakfast places or self-catering apartments and cottages, with a range of US$30-120 per night, while hotels start at US$50 and go up to about US$300.

Opening hours

Most **shops** are open Mon-Fri 0800-1700. If they open on Sat they usually close at 1500. Shops in the malls, however, are open Mon-Sat 1000-1900. Nearly all shops close on Sun and public holidays, but groceries and pharmacies stay open. **Banks** open Mon-Thu 0800-1400, Fri 0800-1300, 1500-1700. Banks in malls open Mon-Fri 1100-1800.

Public holidays

1 Jan New Year's Day
30 Mar Spiritual Baptist Liberation Day
30 May Indian Arrival Day
19 Jun Labour Day
1 Aug Emancipation Day
31 Aug Independence Day
24 Sep Republic Day
25 Dec Christmas Day
26 Dec Boxing Day
In addition there are religious holidays which are public holidays: **Good Friday** and **Easter Monday** in Apr, **Corpus Christi** in Jun, **Eid-Ul-Fitr** in Jun, **Divali** in Oct. The last 2 are announced a couple of weeks before they take place. Most businesses close during Carnival although this is not an official holiday.

Safety

The people of both islands are, as a rule, very friendly but several areas are not safe, especially for women. Most locals are rightly concerned about the level of violent crime and the high murder rate; however, the vast majority of visitors have a safe and enjoyable stay. To the east of Charlotte St, Port of Spain becomes increasingly unsafe. You should avoid Laventille, Morvant and East Dry River. Central Port of Spain is fairly safe, but is quiet at night, apart from around Independence Sq, so exercise caution. Avoid the area around the port or bus terminal except when making a journey.

If you are driving, do not pick anyone up and if you are tailgated, rammed or hit masonry on the road, avoid stopping if at all possible. Robbery and violent crime are the result. Gangs target recent arrivals driving from Piarco airport. Always drive with the doors locked and the windows shut. There have also been incidents of robbery, violence and rape in route taxis and maxi taxis. It is safer to use hotel or pre-booked taxis which charge set fares.

Do not underestimate crime in Tobago. We have received reports of theft and muggings on the Pigeon Point road and parts of Scarborough are known to have crack houses. Do not walk in the Turtle Beach area after dark. There have also been attacks on tourists near waterfalls, on deserted beaches and in other beauty spots. Soft-top jeeps are at risk of theft. Leave nothing in them. Leave your valuables in your hotel safe if you can. Women alone report feeling 'uncomfortable', particularly if they look like a tourist. Violent crime and rape of foreigners has been reported in Tobago. Male and female prostitution has become a problem in Store Bay and elsewhere. HIV infection rates are high on both islands.

Tax

Departure tax, or Passenger Service Charge, is TT$200 (US$32), levied on everyone under the age of 60 when they leave the country. VAT stands at 15% on goods and services. A tax of 10% is levied on all room rates at bed and breakfasts, guesthouses and hotels. Most of them lump tax and service together, charging 21.5% on the rack rate.

Telephone

Country code: 868. The main company providing fixed line and internet services is **TSTT**, www.tstt.co.tt, jointly owned by the government and Cable & Wireless. Its mobile service division is **bmobile**, www.bmobile.co.tt, in line with Cable & Wireless's brand in the region. **Digicel**, www.digiceltt.com, also provides cellular services.

Time

Atlantic Standard Time, 4 hrs behind GMT, 1 hr ahead of EST.

Tipping

If no service charge is included in the bill, tip 10-15% for hotel staff and restaurant waiters; taxi drivers, 10% of the fare, minimum TT$10, but do not tip route taxi drivers. Dockside and airport porters should be tipped about TT$5 for each piece of luggage carried.

Tourist information

Information for visitors is at www. gotrinidadandtobago.com. *Discover Trinidad and Tobago* is published annually and distributed free to all visitors through hotels. **Ministry of Tourism**, Levels 8 & 9, Tower C, International Waterfront Complex, Port of Spain, T6241403, www.tourism. gov.tt, is concerned with policy rather than information. **Tourism Development Company (TDC)**, Level 1, Maritime Centre, 29 Tenth Av, Barataria, T6757034, www.tdc.co.tt, open 0800-1600, is quiet, the pleasant staff have plenty of time to help. They have lists of hotels, restaurants, tour operators, monthly schedule of events, maps for sale, etc. The **office at the airport**, T6695196, daily 0900-2300, is helpful with hotel or guesthouse reservations for your first night (maps of Trinidad and Port of Spain for sale). Elsewhere, it can be difficult to get tourist information. Try **National Carnival Commission**, 11 St Clair Av, St Clair, Port of Spain, T6221670, www.ncctt.org or www.onecarnivalpeople.com and **Division of Tourism and Transportation**, 12 Sangster Hill, Scarborough, Tobago, T6392125, www.visittobago.gov.tt, or at Crown Point Airport, T6390509, or at the cruise ship complex, T6350934.

Useful websites

www.gotrinidadandtobago.com is the general tourist website for both islands; **www.visittobago.gov.tt** is Tobago's tourism website; **www.onecarnivalpeople.com** gives full information on Carnival. **http://discovertnt.com** is the online version of the magazine, *Discover Trinidad and Tobago*.

Vaccinations

No vaccinations are required unless you are coming from a yellow fever area, in which case proof of inoculation is required. However, yellow fever has been reported in monkeys in southern and southeastern Trinidad, so if you are planning to spend time in those rural areas you should consider having a yellow fever vaccination. Immunization against Hepatitis A and Hepatitis B are advised and you should make sure your boosters are up to date for tetanus. See also Health, page 24.

Visas

All visitors are required to have passports, valid for 3 months after your planned departure from Trinidad and Tobago. Visas are not required for visits of under 90 days by nationals of Caricom (except Haiti), most Commonwealth countries, West European countries and the USA. Citizens of some Commonwealth countries do need visas, however. These include Australia, New Zealand, India, Sri Lanka, Nigeria, South Africa, Uganda, Tanzania and Papua New Guinea. Travellers from countries outside the USA and EU must hold a passport valid for 6 months past your travel date, a return ticket and valid visa for entry into Trinidad and Tobago. Applications for entry visas must be submitted to a Trinidad and Tobago Mission abroad or where there is no office, to a British Embassy or Consulate in a non-Commonwealth country. Entry permits for 1 to 3 months are given on arrival; a 1-month permit can be extended at the **Immigration Office**, Head Office at 67 Frederick St, Port of Spain, T6253571, www.immigration.gov.tt, open 0600-1400; visa extensions at 116 Frederick St, T6259261; 2 Knox St, San Fernando, T6536691, 0700-1430; Agricola

Building, Plymouth Rd, Scarborough, T6350430; additional offices in Sangre Grande, Chaguanas and Point Fortin. Your first visit is to make an appointment for a couple of days later; allow several hours for return visit, making sure you take all documents including ticket to home country. The fee varies according to nationality. Try and get a 3-month entry permit if planning a long stay. Business visitors are allowed to work without a work permit for 1 month in any 12 consecutive months.

Even though you may not get asked for it, all travellers need a return ticket to their country of origin, dated, not open-ended, proof that they can support themselves during their stay and an address at which they will be staying in Trinidad (the tourist office at the airport can help). Only those coming from an infected area need a yellow fever inoculation certificate.

Contents

Footprint features

Trinidad

Trinidad is one of the most diverse islands in the Caribbean. Its metropolitan areas are vibrant and it has a great range of natural features to explore. The beautiful, lush northern coast, with its golden beaches, picture-book crescent bays and stunning headlands is backed by densely forested mountains where there is good hiking and excellent birdwatching. Elsewhere there are swamps, mangroves and wetlands, home to innumerable birds from tiny hummingbirds to the magnificent scarlet ibis and other creatures such as manatee or cayman. Another range of hills runs down the centre and along the south, with flat plains in other areas. Forest reserves protect wildlife around the island, preserving habitats and biological diversity. In the south are unusual geological features such as the Pitch Lake, a huge area of tar, and active mud volcanoes.

Trinidad is the economic powerhouse of the twin island nation with its oil and gas industries and its people work hard and play hard. The more extrovert of the two islands, Trinidad is full of energy, from sports to nightlife. Sprawling Port of Spain is the heart of business and finance but the city is known for its cultural and artistic creativity, most dynamically witnessed in Carnival, where music, dance, colour, shape and form whirl together in the parades and parties. Calypso, soca and steel pan were all created here; the urban streets throb with rhythm and beat, while the latest calypsos are matters for debate and political commentary. Unlike most islands in the Caribbean, Trinidad is not dependent on tourism for income and jobs creation, although there are several top-notch hotels, which mainly serve business travellers. There are no all-inclusive tourist enclaves either so it is much easier to experience Trinidadian life and appreciate the genuine warmth of the people.

Port of Spain

Port of Spain lies on a gently sloping plain between the Gulf of Paria and the foothills of the Northern Range. It is a busy port city with constant coming and going of shipping, as well as being an important financial centre and business hub. It is an exciting city, full of life with all the multicultural aspects of Trinidad found here. The capital is renowned for its delicious food and restaurants abound for every conceivable cuisine. Music, from chutney soca to calypso, filters out of clubs and bars into the early hours. A little of the fretwork wooden architecture remains among the modern concrete and office towers; many of the main buildings of interest are within easy reach of the port.

Arriving in Port of Spain → *Country code: 868.*

Getting there

Piarco International Airport is about 16 miles east of the central business district of Port of Spain. Taxi despatchers find taxis for new arrivals; ask to see the notice board or rate card for taxi fares. Unlicensed taxis outside the main parking area charge less, depending on the volume of business, but this is at your own risk and not recommended for safety reasons. Alternatively you can ask your hotel to send a car to collect you. Public transport is some distance away. From the roundabout at the end of the airport terminal approach road you can catch a route taxi to the highway or to Arouca, then take a route taxi or maxi taxi from the junction into Port of Spain but, again, this is not recommended for new arrivals, after dark, if it is raining or if you have luggage. People are very helpful if you need to ask.

Getting around

You can see most of the sights of Port of Spain by walking around the town centre. For further afield, however, there are taxis, buses, route taxis and maxi taxis as well as car hire and ferry.

Tourist information

There are tourist information centres at the airport, the port and at the **Tourism Development Company** (**TDC**) ① *Level 1, Maritime Centre, 29 Tenth Av, Barataria, T6757034, www.tdc.co.tt, open 0800-1600.* They have maps and lots of information and can help with bookings.

Port of Spain was founded in 1757 by the Spanish but, apart from its name, there is not much about the city to recall that era. Street names and place names as well as the historical buildings hark back to the days of the British colony dating from 1797, while skyscrapers and shopping centres reveal the influence of the USA on the modern city.

Trinidad

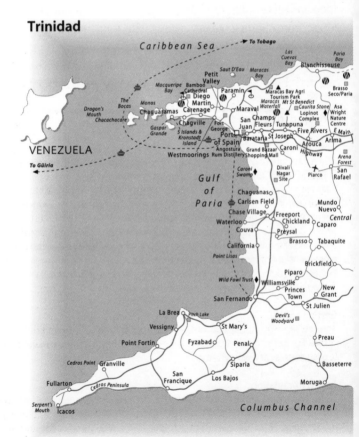

Woodford Square

At the heart of the (rather run down) old city centre is Woodford Square, named after former Governor Sir Ralph Woodford, who developed the town along a square grid plan. On the south side is the fine **Anglican Cathedral Church of the Holy Trinity** (consecrated 1823), with an elaborate hammer-beam roof festooned with carvings. It was built during Woodford's governorship (1813-1828) and contains a very fine monument to him. On the west side of the square, the **Red House** (completed 1907, now undergoing several years of renovation works) contains the House of Representatives (it usually meets on Friday afternoon, you can watch from the public gallery if there is room), the Senate and various government departments. The equivalent of London's Speaker's Corner, you may find dissatisfied members of the electorate outside, haranguing parliamentarians with their grievances. It was the scene of an attempted overthrow of the Robinson Government by armed black Muslim rebels in July 1990. The rebels held the Prime Minister and several of his Cabinet captive for five days before surrendering to the Army. On the west side of the Red House, at the corner of St Vincent and Sackville streets, the former **Police Headquarters**, which the rebels firebombed before launching their assault on the Red House, has been rebuilt. The first Red House on this site was destroyed by fire in 1903 during riots over an increase in water rates. Also in the southwest corner is the striking modern building, the **National Library**, on Hart and Abercrombie, next to the restored Old Fire Brigade Station, which has been incorporated into the new complex. On the opposite side of the square to the cathedral are the modern **Hall of Justice** (it is sometimes interesting to look in and listen to a trial) and the **City Hall**, with a fine relief sculpture on the front.

Government

Trinidad and Tobago became a republic within the Commonwealth on 1 August 1976 under a constitution which provides for a President and a bicameral Parliament comprising a 31-seat Senate and a 36-seat House of Representatives. Tobago has its own 12-seat House of Assembly, which runs many local services. The electoral college which votes for the president is made up of the House of Representatives and the Senate.

Independence Square

On Independence Square (two blocks south of Woodford Square) is the **Roman Catholic Cathedral of the Immaculate Conception**, built on the shoreline in 1832 but since pushed back by land reclamation. The central area of Independence Square, from the cruise ship complex to the cathedral, has been made into an attractive pedestrian area, known as the **Brian Lara Promenade** in honour of the Trinidadian cricketer and former West Indies captain. This is lively in the evening with people liming, drinking beer or playing chess on concrete tables with inlaid chessboards. There are plenty of fast food outlets and vendors selling coconuts or snacks such as doubles. You can often catch a free concert here, with steel pan, soca, jazz or gospel singing. Behind the cathedral is **Columbus Square**, with a brightly painted statue of the island's European discoverer. South of Independence Square, between Edward and St Vincent streets, is the Twin Towers financial complex, two 92-m tall towers, and **Eric Williams Plaza**, housing the Central Bank and Ministry of Finance. A little to the south of the square, the old neoclassical railway station, now known as **City Gate**, is a transport hub for taxis and buses travelling between Port of Spain and eastern Trinidad. Close to the waterfront on South Quay is the **San Andres fort**, built about 1785 to protect the harbour and now an art museum, and a lighthouse which has settled into the ground with a rakish tilt.

Queen's Park Savannah

To the north of the city is Queen's Park Savannah, a large open space with many playing fields and a favourite haunt of joggers. It was the site of Trinidad's main racecourse for decades, until racing was centralized in Arima. In the middle of the Savannah is the Peschier cemetery, still owned and used by the family who used to own the Savannah. Below the level of the Savannah are the **Rock Gardens**, with lily ponds and flowers. Opposite are the **Botanic Gardens** ⓘ *0600-1800, free*, founded in 1818 by Sir Ralph Woodford. There is an amazing variety of tropical and subtropical plants from Southeast Asia and South America, as well as indigenous trees and shrubs. There is very little signage but it is a popular place for a shady walk under the many trees and it is mostly flat. Adjoining the gardens is the small **Emperor Valley Zoo** ① *T6223530, www. zstt.org, 0900-1800 except Christmas Day and Carnival Mon and Tue, no tickets after 1730, US$3.20, children 11 and under half price*, dating from 1952. Initially specializing in animals living wild on the island, with a number of reptiles, including iguanas, boas and the spectacled caiman, there are now caged lions, tigers, giraffes and other non-native species, as well as a butterfly garden. Despite recent upgrading of the facilities, it remains small and cramped for the animals. Also next to the gardens is the presidential residence, a colonial-style building in an 'L' shape in honour of Governor James Robert Longden (1870-1874). Just off the Savannah (on St Ann's Road) is **Queen's Hall** ① *1-3 St Ann's Rd, T6241284, http://queenshalltt.com*, where concerts, shows and other live entertainments are given.

The Magnificent Seven

There are several other Edwardian-colonial mansions along the west side of Queen's Park Savannah on Maraval Road, built in 1904-1910 and known as the Magnificent Seven. The plots for the mansions were sold off after the government moved its farm from St Clair to Valsayn in 1899. The auction in 1902 was specifically for the construction of grand and luxurious mansions. From south to north, they are the Queen's Royal College; Hayes Court, the residence of the Anglican Bishop; Mille Fleurs, or Prada's House (boarded up, awaiting restoration); Roomor or Ambard's House; the Archbishop's Palace; White Hall; and Killarney, also known as Stollmeyer's Castle. Apart from Hayes Court, which was built in 1910, all were built in 1904 and several are now in serious need of restoration.

The **Queen's Royal College** is the most imposing of the Seven, built to a Germanic design at the corner of St Clair and Maraval avenues. It is known for its clock tower, with its chiming clock, as well as for being the leading boys' school on the island. Although it was built to contain six classrooms for 30 boys each, the lecture hall is big enough for 500. After careful restoration, the school now sports its original colours and features from the first part of the 20th century have been preserved.

Hayes Court was built as the official residence for the Anglican bishop and named after Bishop Thomas Hayes, although he died in 1904 before he could take possession of it. It is in relatively good condition, having been well looked after by its occupants, and appears unchanged, although offices for the diocese have been built alongside the main house.

Mille Fleurs, a graceful and elegant house in French provincial style with lovely decorative work, was built as the residence of the Prada family, who occupied it in 1904-1923, after when it was sold to Joseph Salvatori. He and his wife lived there until they both died and their daughter sold the house in

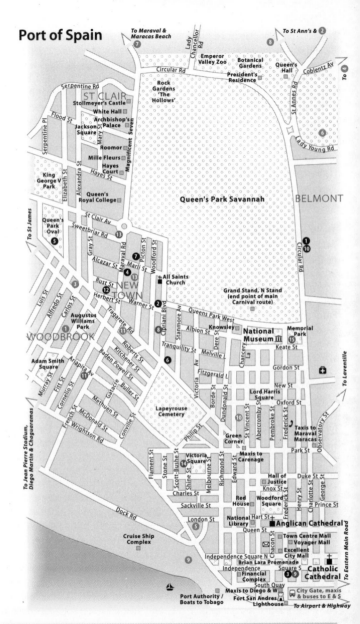

Port of Spain

To Maraval & Maracas Beach

To St Ann's & ②

Lady Chancellor Rd

Emperor Valley Zoo

Botanical Gardens

Queen's Hall

Coblentz Av

To ④

President's Residence

Circular Rd

Rock Gardens 'The Hollows'

St Clair

Serpentine Rd

Stollmeyer's Castle

White Hall

Archbishop's Palace

Jackson Square

Roomor

Mille Fleurs

Hayes Court

Hayes St

Flood St

Serpentine Pl

Mary St

Magnificent Seven

St Annes Rd

Lady Young Rd

⑥

King George V Park

Queen's Royal College

Queen's Park Savannah

BELMONT

Elizabeth St

Alexandra St

To St James

Queen's Park Oval

⑤

St Clair Av

Sweetbriar Rd

⑬

Gray St

Maraval Rd

Picton St

Woodford St

①
⑩

Circular Rd

Alcazar St

Marli St

⑦
④

New Town

Rust St

⑫

Herbert St

Warner St

All Saints Church

Grand Stand, N Stand (end point of main Carnival route)

Luis St

Alfredo St

Carlos St

③

Tragarete Rd

Cipriani Blvd

Stanmore Av

Queens Park West

Grand Stand

Augustus Williams Park

①

Woodbrook

Roberts St

Kitchener St

Baden Powell St

Tranquility St

Albion St

Knowsley

Dere St

Melville L

National Museum 🏛

Memorial Park

⑮

Keate St

Adam Smith Square

Aripita Av

⑪

Murray St

Fitt St

Cornelio St

French St

McDonald St

Galacttic St

Buller St

Methuen St

Conville St

Lapeyrouse Cemetery

Fitzgerald L

Victoria Av

Borde St

Dundonald St

Lord Harris Square

New St

Oxford St

Gordon St

🏥

To Laventille

Wrightson Rd

Phillip St

St Vincent St

Abercromby St

Pembroke St

Frederick St

Park St

Taxis to Maraval Maracas

Observatory St

Flament St

Stone St

Scott-Bushe St

Shine St

Victoria Square

Melbourne St

Richmond St

Edward St

Green Corner

Maxis to Carenage

⑭

Charles St

Sackville St

Red House

Hall of Justice

Knox St

Woodford Square

Duke St

Henry St

Charlotte St

George St

Prince St

Dock Rd

London St

⑤

National Library

Hart St

Queen St

Anglican Cathedral

To Eastern Main Road

Cruise Ship Complex

⑨

Independence Square N

Chacon St

Town Centre Mall

Voyager Mall

Excellent City Mall

Brian Lara Promenade

Independence Financial Complex

South Quay

Independence Square S

③

Catholic Cathedral

Maxis to Diego & W

Port Authority / Boats to Tobago

Fort San Andres Lighthouse

City Gate, maxis & buses to E & S

To Airport & Highway

To Jean Pierre Stadium, Diego Martin & Chaguaramas

N

100 metres
100 yards

1973. It was subsequently bought by the government in 1979 with the aim of making it the offices of the National Security Council, but it is currently unoccupied, boarded up and in an advanced state of deterioration.

Roomor was built for Lucien Ambard and designed by a French architect. It looks like a mini chateau and most of the materials were imported from France, Italy and Scotland. Unfortunately, Ambard could not keep up his mortgage payments and the house was sold and then rented out until Timothy Roodal bought it in 1940. His granddaughter, Dr Yvonne Morgan, now lives in the house and the name is a contraction of Roodal and Morgan. It is the only one of the Seven to be still a private residence and it remains largely as it was when it was built.

The **Archbishop's Palace** was built by the fifth Roman Catholic Archbishop of Port of Spain and has remained in the church ever since. Its Irish architect took Indian styles as his influence, but unfortunate modernization in the 1960s led to a complete remodelling of the ground floor, with concrete walls and aluminium doors replacing the original timbers. Only the first floor, the sacristy and the chapel are in their original state.

White Hall, the largest house, was commissioned by Joseph Leon Agostini, a cocoa planter, who wanted a residence in the Mediterranean style to remind him of his native Corsica. However, the bottom dropped out of the cocoa market, Agostini died in

Religious diversity

Catholics are still the largest religious group but Hindus are not far behind. The Anglican Church and Methodists are also influential, as are many evangelical groups and the Muslim organizations. Spiritual Baptists blend African and Christian beliefs; the women wear white robes and head ties on religious occasions. They can be seen performing baptisms in the sea on the coast to the west of Port of Spain on Sunday nights. Orishas follow a more purely African tradition. Most East Indians are Hindu, some are Muslim, while others have converted to Christianity, particularly Presbyterianism (Canadian Presbyterian missionaries were the first to try converting the Indian population).

1906, and the family could not afford to finish the construction, so in 1907 the property was sold to an American businessman. Robert Henderson lived there with his family and changed its name from the original Rosenweg to White Hall, after giving it a coat of white paint. The house was taken over by US forces during the Second World War until 1944 and then subsequently occupied until 1949 by the British Council, who used it as a cultural centre and sub-let space to libraries and artistic groups. After remaining empty for a few years, it was bought by the government in 1954 and in 1963 became the Office of the Prime Minister, Dr Eric Williams, after Independence. Restored in 2000-2007, it is used as a diplomatic centre and there is no public access.

Killarney was built for Charles Fourier Stollmeyer by a Scottish architect, Robert Gillies, and it may have been designed along the lines of a wing of Balmoral Castle in Scotland. However, the baronial style was too ostentatious for Mrs Stollmeyer and the house was passed on to their son, Conrad. Although occupied by US forces during the Second World War, the house remained in the Stollmeyer family until 1972, when it was sold. In 1979 it became the property of the government but it is in dire need of structural repairs to the roof and floor and lies empty. It is under the care of Citizens for Conservation, http://citizensforconservationtt.org, who have carried out some restoration work.

Around the Savannah

A walk along the north and west sides of the Savannah is best in the early morning (before it gets too hot), arriving outside Queen's Royal College as the students are arriving and the coconut sellers are waking up outside. The **Anglican Church of All Saints** ① *13 Queen's Park West, on the corner with Marli St, www.theanglicanchurchtt.com*, is also worth a visit; it has some fine stained-glass windows. **Knowsley**, another 1904 building, occupies an entire block facing Queen's Park Savannah bounded by Chancery Lane, Dundonald Street and Albion Lane. It was built as the residence of William Gordon Gordon: a massive status symbol, using imported yellow bricks, local coral limestone, marble from Italy for the veranda and green heart timber from Guyana for the magnificent staircase. Since 1956, the building has been owned by the government for the use of the Ministry of Foreign Affairs.

Just off the Savannah, at the corner of Frederick and Keate streets, is the small **National Museum and Art Gallery** ⓘ *117 Frederick St, T6235941, Tue-Sat 1000-1800, Sun 1400-1800, free*, in the former Royal Victoria Institute. It has sections on petroleum and other industries, Trinidad and Tobago's natural history, geology, archaeology and history, carnival costumes, sport and photographs of kings and queens, and art exhibitions (including a permanent exhibition of the work of the 19th-century landscape artist, MJ Cazabon, see also page 20). The exhibitions are tired but comprehensive and the tour is well worthwhile.

Port of Spain suburbs → For listings, see pages 64-82.

The suburbs around Port of Spain vary considerably, some are desirable places to live, others are to be avoided. To the east is **Sea Lots**, a rough squatter area on the shoreline. **Beetham Estate** is even rougher with public housing along the highway. **Laventille** is a working-class hillside suburb, breezy with good views and two big water tanks, **Our Lady of Laventille** and the **Desperadoes** panyard. For a pleasant drive in the hills with attractive views of city, sea and mountains, go up Lady Young Road, about two miles from Savannah, to a lookout 563 ft above sea level (not on a taxi route, but some cars take this route from the airport), or Lady Chancellor Road.

In the northeast, **Belmont** is a run-down but charming area of older housing. **Cascade** is a pretty valley with houses stretching up the hillsides. **St Ann's** is another pretty valley with the Prime Minister's residence (**La Fantasie**) and the psychiatric hospital.

To the northwest, **Newtown** is crowded, commercial and busy, while **St Clair** is spacious, expensive and quiet. **Maraval** is in the next valley with the road running through it to **Maracas** on the coast (heavy rush-hour traffic).

Away from the city centre, to the west of Port of Spain, is the suburb of **Woodbrook**; **Ariapita Avenue** is full of restaurants and pubs, while the suburb of **St James** is known as 'the city that never sleeps'. In Ethel Street there is a large and magnificent Hindu temple, the **Port of Spain Mandir**, known as Paschim Kaashi (Benares of the West). It was built in 1962 for the growing population of Hindus. It contains beautiful *murtis* (statues) imported from India and made especially for the mandir and its lovely garden provides fresh flowers used for worship. On Nepaul Street is the childhood home of writer **VS Naipaul**.

Fort George

From Fort George, a former fort and signal station at 1100 ft, there are also excellent views over the Gulf of Paria as far as the Caroni Swamp and even the hills of Venezuela. The signal station dates from 1802 and the fort was built around 1804 and formerly called **La Vigie**, the 'Lookout', before it was renamed in honour of King George III. The original cannon with his Coat of Arms can still be seen. There were additional fortifications at the foot of the hill at the water's edge and ships on standby. Although it was never used to defend the island, in times of danger people from Port of Spain brought their valuables up here for safe keeping. The fort ceased military operations in 1846. The Victorian signal station you see today was built around 1883 but decommissioned in the 1960s when modern signal towers were built on top of a hill to the north. To reach it take the St James route taxi from Woodford Square and ask to get off at Fort George Road. From there it is about one hour's walk uphill passing through some fairly tough residential territory. You can get a taxi from Bournes Road, St James, if you don't fancy the walk, or take a taxi up and walk down. Go in a group, not alone, as there have been robberies at the Fort. If you have your own car, it is a precarious drive up the hill, but there is plenty of parking space and good rest rooms. There are picnic benches and it is a lovely place to take your lunch or for a romantic spot at sunset.

Around the island

Chaguaramas Peninsula → *For listings, see pages 64-82.*

The Chaguaramas Peninsula is the closest part of Trinidad to South America, a national park whose hills, forests and valleys share many of the features of the mainland. Here you can find red howler monkeys, capuchin monkeys, anteaters, caiman, iguanas, even the occasional ocelot and a host of birds, butterflies and insects. From the hilltops you can get glorious views over the Bay of Paria, the island, its capital and across to Venezuela. Its beaches are popular at weekends and holidays with residents of Port of Spain and its marinas are a safe bolthole from hurricanes further north for a multitude of yachts of all sizes. It is a thriving area for local and foreign tourism with several recent improvements and relatively good security, although this can mean that popular attractions can be crowded.

West to Diego Martin Valley
Midway along the Western Main Road to Chaguaramas a road runs off to the north, through the residential area of Diego Martin. At the north end of the **Diego Martin Valley**, the **Blue Basin Waterfall** and natural landmark, is about a five-minute walk along a path from the road. The area has been cleaned up in recent years, with the removal of much accumulated rubbish and it is a lovely place for a refreshing dip in the pool at the base of the fall, although it can get very crowded at weekends and on public holidays. (Visit the falls in a group if possible to avoid being robbed and leave nothing of value in your car.) At the nearby **River Estate** is a waterwheel dating from 1845 which was once the source of power for a sugar plantation, turning the rollers to crush the cane. Cast iron kettles, part of the boiling process, are on the grass nearby. On the opposite side of the road there is a small museum in a pretty colonial plantation building documenting the history of the cocoa, coffee and sugar industries of the area.

Western Main Road to Chaguaramas
The Western Main Road offers many pretty views, especially of the Five Islands and the nearby Carrera island prison, and runs on past **The Falls at West Mall** in Westmoorings, a huge modern shopping mall in a featureless modern suburb. From here the road continues along the coast past the **Trinidad and Tobago Yacht Club (TTYC)** – opposite Goodwood Park, where the rich live – and to **Carenage**, where there is a fish market and a little church, **St Peter's Chapel**, on the waterside. **St Peter's Day festival**, the first weekend in July, is a mini-Carnival with street parties running late into the night, music and steel pan,

Marinas

Yachting has become big business in Trinidad and there are now several marinas attracting custom from other islands more at risk from hurricanes, with 2000 visiting craft a year. Provisioning is excellent and there are boat repair and maintenance facilities; local teak costs a fraction of US prices, workmen are highly skilled, services are tax-free and spare parts can be imported duty free. Marinas have both dry storage and stern-to docks.

but no costumes. On the Sunday there is a religious service, the original core of the celebration, but now barely visible. A former transhipment facility for Guyanese bauxite is next and then the **Kayak Centre** ① *T6337871, 0600-1800*, which also has mountain bikes. This leads to **Chaguaramas**, on the bay of the same name. On your left is Pier One, a small marina with restaurant and entertainment facilities, popular at weekends, and from where the ferry to Venezuela leaves. Further along are the public beaches of **Williams Bay** and **Chagville Beach** opposite the Chaguaramas Convention Centre. Chagville is a very flat beach and there is usually a breeze, making it popular with windsurfers and kitesurfers. There are changing facilities and toilets. This whole area belonged to the US Navy from 1945 to 1964 but is now under the control of the **Chaguaramas Development Authority (CDA)** ① *T6344364, www.chagdev.com*. Most of the old military buildings are still there, with new uses. Over the last few years the CDA has spent a lot of time and money on improving this stretch of coastline, primarily by re-sanding beaches and constructing a boardwalk in three phases from Williams Bay to Chagville. Restaurants and bars are being encouraged and it is a pleasant area, particularly popular at weekends. The boardwalk is made from recycled plastic, the lighting is solar-powered, there is wheelchair access, seating areas with Wi-Fi hotspots and a good car park. At weekends the western end of the boardwalk and beach is packed with people and the music can be very noisy. The eastern end is usually quieter. There is a bus stop across the road from the beach at Chagville and buses run hourly from Port of Spain.

At the far end of Chagville Beach, the **Chaguaramas Military History and Aerospace Museum** ① *www.militarymuseumtt.com and facebook*, has exhibitions on VE Day and Trinidad's role in both world wars with intricate models as well as relics. The staff are knowledgeable staff, all volunteers, but desperately in need of funding as the museum is under threat of eviction by the CDA.

Next you come to the Sailing Association, Power Boats, Peake's and Industrial Marine Services (IMS), all offering services to the yachting clientele; the area is packed with boats stacked on land or in the water.

Tucker Valley

Just after the police post which marks the start of the old military base, turn right for the Tucker Valley. The old village on the right was emptied to make way for US forces; a half-ruined church and a cemetery can still be seen. The main road leads across the peninsula to a car park, with a concrete path down to the **Macqueripe Beach** in a pretty, wooded bay, with surprisingly good snorkelling. On a clear day you can see the Güiria Peninsula of Venezuela. There is a children's play area, public toilets, changing rooms and picnic tables and benches. There is a lifeguard station, but it isn't always manned. Again, this beach gets crowded at weekends. **Macqueripe Bay** is the location for the area's newest attraction, a zipline and canopy walk run by ZIP-ITT (**Ziplining in Trinidad and Tobago**) **Adventure Tours** ① *T3818543, www.facebook.com/ Trinidadzipitt, Tue-Fri 1000-1600, Sat, Sun and public holidays 1000-1630, 1 hr, US$20*, in conjunction with the CDA. There are seven ziplines and five net bridges/canopy walks, giving you a wonderful view of the bay and the forest.

Turnings to the left from Tucker Valley Road lead to the **Chaguaramas Public Golf Course** ① *http://chaggolfclub.com*, built by US servicemen during their occupation of the peninsula for their own private use. Part of the course was built on the Macqueripe Estate tonka bean plantation and some of the trees still grow there, now well over 100 years old and particularly pretty when in bloom in July and August with a swathe of purple blossom. Golfers may also come across red howler monkeys, caiman, iguanas and many birds while on the course. It became public in 1972 after the US forces left the island and their caddies later formed the golf club; the club house is a good place for a drink. Also from the golf course is the short trail to **Edith Falls**, a nice walk of 20 to 30 minutes through the old tonka bean and cacao plantation, but there is barely a trickle of water in the three-level falls except after heavy rain. Tours are available to both Edith Falls and the Macqueripe Trails (*T6344227, tours@ chagdev.com, US$10, 7-16s US$5*), which are good for finding out more about the fauna and flora of the area.

Another interesting feature, about half a mile from the Tucker Valley Road, is the **Bamboo Cathedral**, also known as Bamboo Cazabon. The almost 1000-ft stretch of bamboo on the Tracking Station Road arches over either side of the road forming a tunnel. In existence for 150 years, it was much painted by the 19th-century artist Michel Jean Cazabon, after whom it has become known.

Offshore islands → *For listings, see pages 64-82.*

The CDA runs tours from its jetty in Chaguaramas by launch (known locally as a *pirogue*) to the offshore islands which dot the Bocas, between Trinidad and Venezuela. On **Gaspar Grande** are the **Gasparee Caves** ① *T6344227,*

Diving off Trinidad

The most varied marine wildlife off Trinidad is found in the channels called the Bocas, between the islands off the northwest peninsula (**The Dragon's Mouth**). However, the currents are cold, so protective gear is essential. At many north coast beaches, particularly **Macqueripe**, a few miles north of the marinas, the diving and snorkelling are safer, if less spectacular. The waters flowing from the Orinoco around Trinidad reduce visibility, but the sea is full of nutrients. There is lots to see but you may not be able to see it, especially in the rainy season.

tours@chagdev.com, US$25, 7-16s US$10, certainly worth a visit. It is about a 20-minute boat ride. The landing stage is at the west end of Gaspar Grande, which has many weekend homes. The caves are about 15 minutes from the landing stage up a good path through woods, quite steep in places and hot. The complex of caves is large but you are only shown one, with good steps leading down and naturally lit from a blow hole. There is a beautiful lake (tidal) at the bottom with stalactites which the guide will light. Parts of the path around the cave are quite slippery. There is no swimming allowed in the cave on crowded days. Take your own food and drink and, although there are toilets, it is a good idea to take your own toilet paper and hand sanitizer. There are also trips to **Scotland Bay** beach (no road access), and to **Chacachacare**, a larger island with ruins of a former leper colony and eight good beaches including nesting sites for the hawksbill turtle. **Boat trips** ⓘ *US$30, US$25 children 7-16*, land at the jetty at La Tinta beach and then you have a guided walk either to the Lighthouse, built in 1896 and still in operation, perched on the highest point of the island with great views, or to the salt pond, a moderate walk. See **Pier One**, page 80, for further details. There are excellent views of the other islands making up the **Dragon's Mouth**. This is much frequented by boats and yachts at the weekend but is virtually deserted during the week. **Monos Island**, at the west tip of Trinidad, has many deep caves and white sandy beaches, popular for weekend homes with more affluent Trinidadians.

North coast → *For listings, see pages 64-82.*

The North Coast Road is stunningly beautiful, running along majestic bays and across hilly promontories and giving access to some of the best beaches on the island. The Northern Range of mountains tumble like crushed green velvet into the Caribbean Sea, providing a safe habitat for wildlife and hiking trails for the intrepid. Maracas Beach is one of the most popular on the island, peaceful and idyllic during the week, turning into a party place at weekends and something of a culinary adventure. The road peters out at Blanchisseuse and it is not possible to drive the length of the north coast.

Port of Spain to Maracas Bay

From Queen's Park Savannah take the road to Maraval and Maracas Bay for about half a mile, then turn right into La Sieva Road just after KFC and RBC. Head north for about 2½ miles passing Morne Coco Road to reach **Maraval**. Just beyond Maraval is the 18-hole **St Andrews golf course** ⓘ *T6290066, http://golftrinidad.com*, at **Moka**. To get there, keep straight on along Perseverance Road. At the fork in the road bear right on to Moka Main Road then turn left at St Andrews Wynd where there is a sign for the golf club. At the end of the road is the security booth where they can direct you to the club house or the pro shop. The golf club has been here since 1891, nestled between the hills in a very picturesque location. The course is well maintained and the club house offers good snacks (bake-and-shark) and liquid refreshment. There is also a swimming pool for which non-members pay a fee to use.

From Maraval village (church, police station) 4WD taxis run to the hilltop village of **Paramin**, where several families still speak French Creole, and there is an annual Parang music festival before Christmas (see Music, page 19). There is a hiking route across the Northern Range from the Santa Cruz Valley, a well-marked trail from Gasparillo village (not to be confused with Gasparillo near San Fernando, Gasparillo can be reached by route taxi from San Juan). The Northern Range locations for hiking are best reached from the coastal villages.

The North Coast Road branches left off Saddle Road (which runs through Maraval back over the hills to meet the Eastern Main Road at San Juan), leading to Maracas Bay, Las Cuevas and Blanchisseuse. As you come over the range you get a magnificent view of the heavily indented bays of the north coast and the rocks and islets offshore. The largest of these is Saut D'Eau Island, off Medine Point, which is a nesting site for brown pelicans, swifts and wood rails. There is a lookout point on the road to Maracas Bay at the **Hot Bamboo Hut**, where a track goes steeply down to a secluded beach on **La Vache Point** and you can explore **Balata Bay**. The stall-holder can call the toucans in the forest. Take binoculars to see them fly close and answer him. There are many stalls along the road offering fruit, snacks, drinks and handicrafts to weekend visitors from Port of Spain.

Maracas Bay

Some 10 miles from the capital, Maracas Bay has a sheltered sandy beach fringed with coconut palms. Despite small waves there can be a dangerous undertow here and at other beaches, and drownings have occurred; do not swim far out and watch the markers. Swim at the east end away from the river

Rainforests

The **Northern Range Sanctuary**, Maracas, or **El Tucuche Reserve**, is a forest on the second-highest peak, at 3072 ft, covering 2313 acres. The slopes are covered with forest giants such as the silk cotton trees, which carry creepers and vines. The thick forest canopy of mahogany, balata, palms and flowering trees like the poui and immortelle provides cover and maintains a cool, damp environment no matter the heat of the day. The interesting flora and fauna include giant bromeliads and orchids, the golden tree frog and the orange-billed nightingale-thrush. There are several hiking trails, the most popular of which is from Ortinola estate (Maracas, St Joseph valley, which is on other side of mountains from Maracas beach; guides can be hired. The seven-mile trek to the peak takes five hours through dense forest; the views from the top are spectacular; for information on hiking contact the **Field Naturalists' Club** (http://ttfnc.org). Much easier is the three-hour trail to Maracas beach from Gasparillo village in Santa Cruz, not to be confused with Gasparillo near San Fernando. The trail is kept clear by a job-creation scheme and is easy to follow.

mouth. It can be very crowded on Sundays and holidays with loud music and parties down the far end of the beach, but fairly quiet otherwise. It is also the place people come on Ash Wednesday to relax after the rigours of Carnival. Lifeguards are on duty until 1800; there are changing rooms (TT$1), showers, beach chairs etc, car parking and cabanas for beach vendors. This is the place to come for bake-and-shark; opinions vary over which stall sells the best. **Richard's** is the most famous, but **Mom's** is reputed to serve the best fish and **Natalie's** the crispiest bake. All offer sauces and a buffet station of vegetables and salads as toppings to customize your meal. You don't have to eat shark; there are other fish, shrimp or even vegetarian options. There are route taxis from Park Street, Port of Spain, but all transport is irregular and infrequent. It is easy at weekends to reach but less so during the week. Difficulties in catching the bus have led travellers to recommend car hire or taxis.

If you turn inland after the bake-and-shark vendors on the Grand Fond Road, on your left is the **Maracas Bay Agri Tourism Park** ① *T3050489, www.maracasbayagritourismpark.com, Wed-Sun 1030-1830, TT$30 for Trinis, US$20 for foreigners*, showcasing local types of farming, such as sugar cane, orchard fruits, aquaculture, as well as native fauna and flora. There is also a mini-golf course, a caiman pond, fishing, you can camp overnight and they organize bonfire limes from time to time, among other activities.

North coast beaches

Next to Maracas Bay is **Tyrico Bay** (surfing, lifeguard), another horseshoe-shaped beach with undertow, which is quieter than Maracas and has greyish-brown sand. **Las Cuevas** (changing rooms, showers, lifeguards, surfing at the far end occasionally, beware of the sandflies in the wet season), about five miles from Maracas Bay, is a picturesque bay with a wide sandy beach, calm waters popular with families and fishing boats moored at the east end. The west end is very beautiful but can be isolated, so it is best to go in groups. It is busy on Sunday but quiet during the week. The bay gets its name from the Spanish word for caves, of which there are many along the edge.

There are smaller beaches beyond **La Fillette** and at **Blanchisseuse**. Blanchisseuse is divided between the Upper Village and Lower Village, with the Arima road as the dividing line. There is a post office, health centre, Roman Catholic Church, government offices and police station in Lower Village, while Upper Village has the recreation field, school and several artisans working in wood and leather. Leatherback turtles come on to Blanchisseuse beach in the nesting season.

At **Marianne Bay**, at the far end of Blanchisseuse, the beach has a sweet water lagoon where the river runs into the sea. This is a popular place for river bathing but watch out for sandflies and for mosquitoes at dusk. The place is kept clean by the owners of **Cocos Hut restaurant/Laguna Mar Beach Resort**, who have established a 28-acre nature reserve on the banks of the river.

Marianne River is dramatically beautiful with overhanging vines, buttress roots of trees, boulders and pools, and lots of birds. You can either hike up the river or rent a kayak. About 40 minutes upriver you reach the Three Pools, beautiful bathing spots. Beyond these pools, with their natural slides and jacuzzis, you need a guide to reach Avocat Falls, which are spectacular. Eric Blackman (T6693995, owner of **Northern Sea View Villa**) has kayaks to rent, and offers two-hour tours to the pools and all-day tours to the falls.

All this part of the coast is very beautiful with the forest tumbling down to the sea. The paved road continues to some luxury villas across the suspension bridge over the Marianne River but then peters out and is little more than a rutted dirt track, formerly used as a donkey trail to service the old cocoa plantations along the way. The bridge was made in Glasgow in 1898 and first installed in Mayaro, but moved to Blanchisseuse and reassembled in 1955-1956. You can hike east all along the coast from here to Paria Bay, Matelot and on to Grande Riviere, starting at the suspension bridge just outside the village. It can be done in a day, or two if overnighting in Paria and a guide is useful; ask Fred Zollna (at **Laguna Mar**) or Eric Blackman to arrange it.

From Arima you can drive or take a taxi to Brasso Seco and Paria. From here the trail runs to **Paria Bay**, possibly the best beach on the island (can be littered after public holidays), about eight miles, ask directions, or see the **TIDCO Sites** (trail guide) book for the route. There is a primitive shelter on the beach but no other facilities so take provisions with you. At the beach, turn right to get to the bridge over the Paria River, from where it is a five-minute walk inland to the spectacular Paria waterfall. Another path from the beach leads west to Blanchisseuse seven miles). Leatherback turtles nest along all this part of the coast, but its isolation means that it is also used by those with less benign intent, such as drug smugglers. Hiking is safest at weekends or in a group. People hike to Paria Bay from Blanchisseuse in a couple of hours, but it would take you all day at a good pace to reach Matelot, so most camp overnight on the beach. Carry plenty of water and a picnic for a day trip.

East of Port of Spain to Arima → For listings, see pages 64-82.

The east–west corridor from Port of Spain is a line of industrial and residential suburbs linked by the Eastern Main Road and, more quickly, by a dual carriageway or priority bus/taxi route. Although the flat bits are mostly unattractive, you are never more than a mile or two from the hills and both high- and low-income neighbourhoods extend up the hillsides, with wonderful views of Central Trinidad and across to the Gulf of Paria. The older centres along the Eastern Main Road, San Juan, Curepe, Tunapuna, Arouca, are lively, with shops, small bars, Chinese restaurants and fruit and vegetable markets, the latter jamming up the traffic even on Sunday morning.

Angostura Rum Distillery
ⓘ *T6231841 ext 255/257, www.angostura.com, tours Mon-Fri 0930 or 1300, US$10, book 3 days in advance, groups preferred.*
Just east of Port of Spain on Eastern Main Road, after the coconut processing factory, is the Angostura rum distillery. It sits on a 20-acre site, with its colour-coded stills towering up like an oil refinery. The tour begins with a short film on the history of the company and its famous bitters, a visit to the Angostura museum and one-of-a-kind Barcant Butterfly Collection and a behind-the-scenes tour of the 'Bitters Manufacturing Room'. Visitors can then ride on an open-air tram down to the state-of-the-art rum distillery and bottling plant, followed by rum tasting and shopping. Angostura Ltd is one of the Caribbean's foremost rum producers whose portfolio includes award-winning and internationally acclaimed rum brands such as 1824, 1919, Single Barrel Reserve, Reserva, 5 Year Old and 7 Year Old. It is also the world's market leader for its Angostura aromatic bitters, the recipe for which has not been changed since its inception in 1824 and for which there is a royal warrant to the Queen. They also make a non-alcoholic drink known as LLB (Lemon, Lime and Bitters).

To St Joseph

At **Champs Fleurs** is the **Carib brewery**, and then the Mount Hope teaching hospital. **St Joseph** was once the seat of government, as San José de Oruña. The imposing **Jinnah Memorial Mosque** stands here. Completed in 1954, the green and white mosque is named after the founder of Pakistan, Quaid-I-Azam Mohammed Ali Jinnah. In the centre, the 24-ft-high main dome is 40 ft in diameter, surrounded by glass louvres and crowned by the crescent and star. Four half domes around the main dome each have a door allowing onlookers to see both the inside of the dome and the prayer hall on the ground floor, which can hold some 600 worshippers. Beyond them, six small domes with spires stand at the corners of the hexagonal structure and on the very outside are two tall minaret towers, also capped with domes.

Maracas Valley

North of St Joseph is the Maracas Valley (no road to Maracas Bay, although there is a footpath). People refer to the area as Maracas-St Joseph to distinguish it from Maracas Beach on the other side of the mountains. The valley was one of the first areas to be settled and the Maracas Royal Road running up the valley is one of the oldest roads on the island. The river running through it is called the **Saint Joseph River** or the **Maracas River** and is a major tributary of the Caroni River. A pleasant area, its main tourist attraction is a 300-ft waterfall, reached by a good trail 20 minutes from Waterfall Road. It weaves through the forest with its myriad plants, birds and butterflies until you get to a pretty glade. In the dry season the waterfall is like smoke cascading down the rocks, but in the wet season it is more impressive and you can bathe in the pool at its foot. However, in 2014 the waterfall was under threat because of plans to build a dam, reservoir and sediment trap on the river for flood prevention, which would make the waterfall inaccessible and leave many homes on Waterfall Road under water.

Mount St Benedict Monastery

Further east, high on a hill, is Mount St Benedict Monastery (the oldest Benedictine complex in the Caribbean), reached through St Johns Road in St Augustine. Although the monastery was founded by a Belgian, the first Benedictine monks came from Bahia, Brazil, in 1912. It started with a tapia hut but construction of the main building on Mount Tabor began in 1918. The monastery has a retreat, lots of educational facilities, a drug rehabilitation centre, a farm and a guesthouse and is popular with birdwatchers and walkers. The little café at the guesthouse does good afternoon tea and they make their own yoghurt, for sale in the shop, with tropical flavours: guava, soursop, pineapple, almond, and more. There are marvellous views over the Caroni Plain to the sea and a picnic area from which to enjoy them. A white van shuttle service (TT$4, US$0.60), marked St Benedict Monastery, leaves from outside Scotia Bank on

St John's Road, corner of Eastern Main Road, in Tunapuna every 30 minutes to the top of the hill. A priority maxi taxi from Port of Spain to St Augustine takes 20 minutes, then a route taxi up St John's Road and then St Michael's Road will take you close to the monastery, but unless you pay to go off route it is still a stiff walk uphill. Otherwise take a private taxi all the way. From Caura Road, a little further east, a route taxi will take you up the valley of the Caura River, where the pools are popular spots for weekend picnics (river limes).

Lopinot Complex

A little further along the Eastern Main Road at Arouca, the road branches south to Piarco International Airport, or north winding six miles up into the forested mountains to the Lopinot Complex, an estate built by the Comte de Lopinot (see page 53) at the turn of the 19th century. Originally called La Reconnaissance, it is now a popular picnic spot and destination for school trips, well-maintained by the Forestry Division. There is also a small museum. It hosts a Parang music festival before Christmas and parang music is played in the museum when there are visitors. There is a bar across the road, open, like most others in Trinidad, 'anyday, anytime' and the Café Mariposa for lunch or dinner close by in Lopinot. The river is a short walk away if you want to cool down.

Caurita Stone

High on a ridge in the Maracas Valley are the only known Amerindian petroglyphs in Trinidad, drawings on a stone known as the Caurita Stone. They show a series of faces with curving lines indicating limbs; some have been identified as a chief, other people in ceremonial garb, and a deer. The stone is roughly 6 ft high by 8 ft wide and the drawings are on the top half where it is exposed. You may need to clear off moss if no one has visited for a while. The Santa Rosa Carib Community (see below) regard the stone as having special spiritual significance and often visit for their ceremonies when shamans give offerings. To get there it is a stiff climb of one to 1½ hours in the valley, with access from the main crossroads between San Juan and Tunapuna. The trail winds through forest and coffee and cocoa estates, criss-crosses a little stream and offers great opportunities for bird watching; you can see oropendolas' nests in the immortelle trees.

Arima

Arima is 16 miles east of Port of Spain, reached by bus or route taxi. The landmark at the centre is the **Dial**, an old public clock donated to the town by the mayor in 1898 after he bought it in Nice, France. It was repaired after an argument with a heavy truck several years ago, but no longer chimes. Arima is also known for its 18th-century Santa Rosa Roman Catholic Church, whose statue of the Virgin Mary allegedly started crying tears of blood. On the last Sunday in August it is the location for the annual feast of Santa Rosa de Lima.

Roman Catholic immigration

The first Spanish Governor was Don Antonio Sedeño who arrived in 1530 but who failed to establish a permanent settlement because of Indian attacks. In 1592 Governor Don Antonio de Berrio y Oruna, founded the town of San José de Oruna (now St Joseph). It was destroyed by Sir Walter Raleigh in 1595 and not rebuilt until 1606. In 1783 a deliberate policy to encourage immigration of Roman Catholics was introduced, known as the Royal Cedula of Population, and it was from this date that organized settlement began with an influx of mostly French-speaking immigrants, particularly after the French Revolution. Many also came from St Lucia and Dominica when these islands were ceded to Britain in 1784. Others came with their slaves from the French Caribbean when slavery was abolished and from Saint Domingue after the War of Independence there (including the Compte de Lopinot, whose house in Lopinot has been restored, see page 52).

Arima is the focus of Trinidad's Amerindian heritage and still has a recognized Carib community. The town was founded in 1757 when Capuchin monks arrived to convert the local people to Christianity and many were relocated here when their lands were seized in 1783 for cocoa plantations. A group of people regard themselves as descendants of the original Amerindians of the area, although there are none left of pure blood. They have a figurehead Carib queen and call themselves the **Santa Rosa Carib Community**. They celebrate an annual heritage event at the end of August, which usually coincides with the Roman Catholic festivities and the city's Borough Day celebrations.

West of the church in the centre of town is the Santa Rosa Carib Community Crafts Centre selling traditional crafts: cassava squeezers, serving trays, carvings, etc. A few miles west of Arima is a small but interesting **Amerindian museum** ① *0600-1800, free but donations are welcome*, at the Cleaver Woods Recreation Park, housed in a reproduction Amerindian long house.

North of Arima → *For listings, see pages 64-82.*

Asa Wright Nature Centre (AWNC)
① *T6674655, www.asawright.org, 0900-1700, non-residents US$10 (TT$60) entrance and tour, children 12 and under US$6, advance reservations required. Buffet lunch in the dining room 1200-1300, Mon-Sat US$23/TT$140, Sun US$33/TT$200, children half price, sandwiches on the veranda 1100-1600,*

Flora and fauna

The rainforests of the **Northern Range** running along the north coast and the wetlands on the east and west coast are more extensive, more dense and display a greater diversity of fauna and flora than any other ecosystems in the Caribbean. The **Forestry Division** (Long Circular Rd, St James, Port of Spain, T6224521, information on guided tours and hikes) has designated many parts of Trinidad and Tobago as national parks, wildlife reserves and protected areas. On Trinidad, the national parks are the Caroni and Nariva Swamps, Matura and Chaguaramas.

Many flowering trees can be seen on the islands: pink and yellow poui, frangipani, cassia, pride of India, immortelle, flamboyant, jacaranda. Among the many types of flower are hibiscus, poinsettia, chaconia (wild poinsettia – the national flower), ixora, bougainvillea, orchid, ginger lily and heliconia. The **Horticultural Society of Trinidad and Tobago** (PO Box 252, Lady Chancellor Road, T6226423) has its office in Port of Spain.

The islands are home to 60 types of bat, and other mammals include the Trinidad capuchin and red howler monkeys, brown forest brocket (deer), collared peccary (quenk), manicou (opossum), agouti, rare ocelot and armadillo. A small group of manatees is being protected in a reserve in the Nariva Swamp. Other reptiles include iguanas and 47 species of snakes, of which few are poisonous: the fer-de-lance (locally, *mapipire*), bushmaster and two coral snakes. The variety of fauna on Tobago is larger than on other similar-sized islands because of its one-time attachment to South America. It is home to 210 different bird species, 123 different butterfly species, 16 types of lizards, 14 kinds of frogs, 24 species of snakes (all of them harmless), and it has some spectacled caymans at Hillsborough Dam.

Trinidad and Tobago together have more species of birds than any other Caribbean island, although the variety is South American, not West Indian. No species is endemic, but Tobago has 13 species of breeding birds not found on Trinidad. Some estimates say that there are 433 species of bird, including 41 hummingbirds, parrots, macaws, the rare red-breasted blackbird, the nightingale-thrush and the motmot. There are also 622 recorded species of butterfly. The most accessible birdwatching sites are the **Caroni Bird Sanctuary**, the **Asa Wright Centre**, the Caurita Plantation and the **Wild Fowl Trust**.

accommodation available. Car or taxi from Arima, the driver should wait for you, or a warm 2½-hr walk uphill through lovely forests; taxi from Port of Spain will wait 1½ hrs, US$80/TT$480.

About eight miles north of Arima, off the Blanchisseuse Road, you can get to the Asa Wright Nature Centre, an old plantation house for the former cocoa/coffee/citrus Spring Hill Estate overlooking a wooded valley and a must for bird-lovers. The nature centre now owns nearly 1500 acres of protected forest (not all of which are at the centre) and 166 species of birds can be seen here. There is a beautiful man-made pool where you can swim, a network of trails and guided tours. Sit on the veranda and watch the hummingbirds while you have a sandwich and drink – sublime. Take binoculars and a camera, the hummingbirds are not camera shy; wear insect repellent but no perfume and wear neutral colours. The rangers are very knowledgeable and can tell you about the plants and insects (easier to see) as well as the birds. The rare oilbirds in **Dunstan Cave** (also called Diablotin Cave) can only be seen if you stay more than three nights.

Field trips for guests are organized to the Caroni Swamp, Nariva Swamp, Aripo Savannah, Arena Forest and Blanchisseuse, while turtle-watching tours are also offered to the east and west coasts during leatherback nesting season (March to September). In 2013, the Centre opened the Richard ffrench Natural History Museum to coincide with the launch of the third edition of the *Guide to the Birds of Trinidad and Tobago* by Richard ffrench. The museum contains his handwritten notes and papers gathered during his life as well as botanical and zoological exhibits.

The road to the nature centre carries on to Blanchisseuse, see page 49. A nine-mile walk from the road are the **Aripo Caves** (the longest system in Trinidad at 2828 ft in length and 525 ft deep) with spectacular stalagmites and stalactites (in the wet season, June to December, a river runs through the caves). Oilbirds can be seen at the entrance and there are bats. Only fully equipped spelunkers should venture beyond the entrance. To get there, turn at Aripo Road off the Eastern Main Road, turn right at the four mile post, over the bridge into Aripo village. Keep left, continuing uphill to a wide bend to the left where you may park off the road and begin the walk uphill. Turn left at the small house. After a further 10 minutes take the trail to the right of the junction and to the left at the next junction, continuing uphill along the river. At a shelf of rock there is a well-cleared trail away from the river. Keep to this trail heading north until the top of the hill. Go downhill for five minutes to the stream leading into the cave. A guide is advised or join a group such as **Island Hikers**, www.islandhikers. com; Mario, one of their group leaders, can arrange a private hike, T7492956.

Northeast coast → *For listings, see pages 64-82.*

The northeast coast is one of the most remote and unspoiled parts of the island, partly because the road does not extend along the whole of the north coast from Blanchisseuse. It is time-consuming to get there, but worth it for the

Leatherback turtles

The leatherback turtle nests from March to September on several beaches on Trinidad (Matura, Fishing Pond on east coast, Paria, Tacaribe and Grande Riviere on north coast) and Tobago (Great Courland Bay known as Turtle Beach, Stonehaven Bay, Bloody Bay and Parlatuvier), up to eight times a season, laying 75 to 120 eggs, each time about 10 days apart. Incubation is 60 days.

peace and serenity. Long stretches of sand attract nesting leatherback turtles and numerous birds and butterflies live in the forest dipping its toes in the sea.

From Arima east to Toco

If you are driving, from Arima the road runs either to **Toco** at Trinidad's northeast tip or, branching off at Valencia, to the east coast. The journey to Toco has some interesting places to visite en route. Take the left fork at **Valencia**, then left again at **Honey Corner** (where there are bottles of locally made honey on sale), through small villages, woods and, after Salybia, there are some beaches a short distance off the road to the right. The **Salybia Waterfall** is close to the 13 mile post; cross the bridge and turn left after the old 14¼ mile post into the Salybia/Matura Trace. Follow a 20-minute, rather rough drive and park in front of two houses. Walk 15 minutes along the trail, turn left at the junction, continue about 10 minutes to a second junction where the path narrows on the right going slightly uphill into Mora Forest. Keep on the trail, crossing first a small stream and then a larger river. Some 10 minutes later at another junction you may bear right over a small hill or walk upstream. Either route will get you to Salybia Waterfall and pool in 10 minutes. The waterfall is not very high but the pool is 20 ft deep and recommended for good swimmers. There is also a picnic area.

At **Galera Point**, reached off the road which goes to Toco, over a rickety wooden bridge, there is a small, pretty lighthouse marked with Queen Victoria's initials. If you arrive before 1530 it is often open and you can climb to the top for a breathtaking view from the ramp. Even if it is closed, it is worth stopping for a picnic and to admire the views. Tobago can be seen from here. The waves can be impressive, crashing against the rocks and forming blowholes.

Toco is well worth a visit with a few small beaches nearby for bathing, and from here you can continue by car (quite a long drive) to Grande Riviere.

Grande Riviere

Grande Riviere lies in the middle of this area, a small village with a population of only 300. It has a long and lovely beach, with accommodation and eco-tourism. Guesthouses can organize birdwatching or hiking tours into the forest and along the path to Blanchisseuse. It is believed to be the largest nesting site for the leatherback turtle in the Western Hemisphere and in season (March-August) you can watch the protected turtles laying their eggs in the sand, then later (May-September) see the thousands of hatchlings dig their way out of the nests and make their way to the sea. There is a wide river, also good for bathing, and hiking trails in the hills behind.

Grande Riviere is easy to reach by private car but not easy by public transport. From Port of Spain take a bus (faster than a maxi) to Arima, US$0.65. From Arima to Sangre Grande there are buses and maxis (ask around) but a route taxi may be easiest; turn left just past **Scotia Bank** and the third lot of route taxis is for Sangre Grande. At Sangre Grande buses, maxis and route taxis all stop in the same place. It is relatively easy to get a maxi to Toco and possibly on to Sans Souci, but this still means a six-mile walk (very pleasant, no traffic) through the woods to Grande Riviere. There are some maxis and route taxis in the morning from Grande Riviere to Sangre Grande, returning at about 1600. As a last resort a route taxi in Sangre Grande would very soon become a private taxi. Guesthouses at Grande Riviere can also arrange to pick you up, price negotiable. Whichever way you go, the effort is worthwhile.

East coast → For listings, see pages 64-82.

The Atlantic coast from Matura to Mayaro is divided into three huge sweeping bays, with enormous palm trees in some places. Of these bays **Mayaro** and **Manzanilla** both have beautiful sandy beaches, but the Atlantic currents can make swimming dangerous. There are several beach houses to rent at Mayaro, heavily booked in peak holiday periods; some are poor, so check beforehand. Manzanilla has public facilities and a hotel. From nearby **Brigand Hill Lighthouse**, a TSTT signal station, you can get a wonderful view of the east coast, the Nariva Swamp and much of Trinidad. Light patches of green are rice fields encroaching illegally on the swamp.

The **Nariva Swamp**, the largest freshwater swamp in Trinidad, is a Wetland of International Importance under the Ramsar Convention. It contains hardwood forest and is home to red howler monkeys and the weeping capuchin as well as 55 other species of mammal of which 32 are bats. There are also manatee, protected in a reserve. Birds include the savannah hawk and the red-breasted blackbird. A tour by kayak is recommended (see page 79 for details) as you will see more than you would on a motor boat. You paddle silently across fields of giant water lilies, through channels in the thick forest of mangroves and towering silk cotton trees, with monkeys and parrots chattering overhead.

South of Port of Spain → For listings, see pages 64-82.

Driving south from Port of Spain along the Uriah Butler highway, you will see sugar, citrus and rice fields, maybe a few buffalypso (buffaloes which have been selectively bred for meat), and Hindu temples and mosques. The great attraction of this stretch of coast is the Caroni Swamp, where egrets and the spectacular scarlet ibis arrive at dusk to roost, a beautiful mix of red and white perched in the green trees against the blue sky and then a glorious sunset.

Caroni Bird Sanctuary
The bird sanctuary is a lagoon, part of the Caroni Swamp, a Wetland of International Importance under the RAMSAR Convention. A two-hour boat trip into the Caroni Bird Sanctuary (poorly signposted from the highway), the home of scarlet ibis (*Eudocimus ruber*), is a fascinating experience. Tours take place in the late afternoon so that you can see thousands of the scarlet ibis, herons and egrets returning to their roost at dusk. Guides on board your boat will also point out other wildlife, from birds such as eagles and parrots, to crabs, fish and boas living in the mangroves. Numbers of scarlet ibis have declined as the swamp in which they live has been encroached upon, but this is still a magical sight; the trees appear to turn red as groups of up to 20 birds arrive together and settle down for the night. Boats leave around 1600 from near the Visitor's Centre to take people to see the ibis returning to their roost at sunset. There are two boat operators in the swamp: **Moodoo Tours** ① *T6630458, www.madoobirdtours.com*, and **Nanan's Tours** ① *T6451305, www.nanan ecotours.com, US$10, group rates and transport available, also kayaking and fishing tours*. You can also enquire at the **Asa Wright Nature Centre** (page 53) for more detailed tours. You might like to take a cold bag with drinks. Mosquito repellent is essential when you get off the boat at the end of your trip.

To get there, take a bus or route taxi from Port of Spain or San Fernando to Bamboo Grove Settlement No 1, on the Uriah Butler Highway, from where the boats leave. Maxi taxi (green bands) leave from Independence Square; ask to be dropped off at the Caroni Bird Sanctuary.

South to San Fernando
On the left before you get to **Chaguanas**, a large blue statue of the Hindu god, Lord Shiva and a large white statue of Viveka Nanda, a Hindu philosopher, mark the site of the annual **Divali Nagar exhibition** in October/November. The village of **Felicity** on the west of Chaguanas is famous for its elaborate Divali celebrations.

Chaguanas (population 62,000) is a busy place, not an architectural must, but full of bargains for the shopper and there are several malls. At the centre is the imaginatively named junction Busy Corner. The **Lion House** (on the main road to the east, close to the police station) is the original for VS Naipaul's *A House for Mr Biswas*.

Continuing south on the Southern Main Road parallel to the highway, **Carlsen Field** has several small potteries, using open wood-fired kilns. Most of the pots are a bit unwieldy, but wind chimes, etc are easily portable, as are the tiny lamps, or *deyas*, which are made for Divali.

Turn off the Main Road at Chase Village, and three miles to the west is **Waterloo**, where a small white and blue Hindu temple has been built in the sea. It is reached by a short causeway and it is the successor of a structure built by Siewdass Sadhu, a sugar worker who selected his site in the shallow waters of the Gulf of Paria after being unable to find land to build on. There is no guard or anyone to give information. Cremations are carried out on the shore and you may come across a funeral in progress or notice the after-effects of the burning pyre. When the tide is out, the mud and garbage revealed can be unsightly and smelly. Close by is the **Dattatreve Centre** with an impressive Hanuman *murti* (statue), the largest *murti* built outside India. Continuing south, the Southern Main Road leads to the Point Lisas industrial estate.

Alternatively, a left turn-off the highway at **Freeport**, or points south, takes you into the Central Range through sugar and citrus fields, then forests, with cocoa trees. There are cocoa houses with a sliding roof so that the beans can dry in the sun but go under cover when it rains. Pretty little villages with wooden houses and well-kept gardens overflow with hibiscus and bougainvillea. The roads are narrow and winding, so unless you are a map-reading wizard, you are bound to get lost. At **Chickland Village** near Freeport, the **Ajoupa Pottery** ① *T6730605, www.ajoupapottery.com*, with a wooden 19th-century estate house, is well worth a visit to see the grounds, mosaics and statues. The gardens are open Saturday and Sunday 1000-1800, but phone in advance. Bunty O'Connor, a potter, runs workshops and offers writers and artists a retreat.

San Fernando

San Fernando ('Sando' to locals) on the southwest coast is a busy, hot city, as yet unspoilt by tourism but spoilt by just about everything else. It is the centre of industry on the island, surrounded by oil, gas and petrochemical refineries, iron and steel and aluminium smelters. A highway connects Port of Spain with San Fernando, making it a 30-minute drive (90 minutes in the afternoon rush hour, quicker by ferry, see page 10). The waterfront area is a mess, in spite of continual talk of restoration, although Harris Promenade is pleasant. City Hall, the Our Lady of Perpetual Help Church and the old railway engine are worth a look. Library Corner has the old Carnegie public library and is the main centre for maxis and route taxis. Coffee Street is also lively.

Above the city is **San Fernando Hill**, oddly shaped as a result of quarrying and easily picked out from Northern Range viewpoints or from Chaguaramas. It is now landscaped, and you can either walk or drive to the top for a spectacular view. Carib House, on Carib Street, is a popular landmark on San Fernando Hill. It was built by a Barbadian stonemason called Samuel Atherly, who used brick ballast for the ground floor pillars, and who also built the local court house and police station in the 1870s.

Pointe-a-Pierre Wild Fowl Trust

North of San Fernando are the principal industrial area of **Point Lisas** and the PETROTRIN oil refinery. Within the oil refinery is the 26-ha **Pointe-a-Pierre Wild Fowl Trust** ① *T658 4200, ext 2512, www.papwildfowltrust.org, Mon-Fri 0900-1700, Sat, Sun 1000-1700, reservations essential to get you through security*, a conservation area with two lakes and breeding grounds for many endangered species, an interesting museum and interactive centre. Many birds bred in captivity are later released into the wild. Call 48 hours in advance to get permission to enter the compound (many entrances, it can be confusing).

Pitch Lake

① *TT$30/US$5, maxi taxi from the wharf in San Fernando to La Brea and say you want to get off at the Pitch Lake (TT$10/US$1.60. To get back, take a route taxi, bus or maxi from in front of the garage).*

A famous phenomenon to visit on the southwest coast just after La Brea is the Pitch Lake, some 116 acres of smooth black tar; it is 135 ft deep and the largest natural asphalt lake in the world. It is possible to walk on it, with care, watching out for air holes bubbling up from the pressure under the ooze. It is perfectly safe with a guide but dangerous without. In the wet season, however, most of the area is covered with shallow fresh water. The pitch has medicinal value for skin complaints and you can bathe in pools with fish. Cashew trees grow on the pitch and the surrounding land is very fertile.

The legend has it that long ago the gods interred an entire tribe of Chaima Indians for daring to eat sacred hummingbirds containing the souls of their ancestors. In the place where the entire village sank into the ground there erupted a sluggish flow of black pitch, which gradually became an ever-refilling large pool.

Go to the TDC information office inside the car park where you will find an official guide, tip appreciated. Locals who pose as guides outside the entrance harass tourists for large tips. Agree on a price in advance as there are no fixed rates. Sometimes there are crowds of guides who are difficult to avoid, but on the other hand it is difficult to understand the lake without explanation.

Just south of La Brea is **Vessigny beach**, which fills up with people at weekends and is a bit of a party beach. It isn't as pretty as some and can be polluted from local industry, but there are changing facilities and snack bars open at weekends and holiday times.

Southwest peninsula → *For listings, see pages 64-82.*

Beyond La Brea the road continues to **Point Fortin**, a small but busy town with a liquefied natural gas plant and a small beach. The road carries on down the southwest peninsula, deteriorating as it goes, through **Cedros** (fishing village, the widest beach on the island at low tide) past miles of coconut palms to **Icacos**, from which the mangroves of the Orinoco delta are clearly visible a few miles across the water. From the Point Fortin–Icacos road there are side roads leading to beaches such as **Erin** on the south coast where there are lots of fishing boats pulled up on the beach, or **Columbus Bay**, a 2½-mile stretch between Los Gallos Point and Corral Point. Christopher Columbus sailed into the bay on 2 August 1498 and named the point because it looked like a cockerel's comb. Three large rocks jut out from the sea offshore and erosion has created a rock arch in a smaller bay beyond the river.

East of San Fernando → *For listings, see pages 64-82.*

East of San Fernando the main road runs through rolling hills, past the rusting hulk of the **Usine Sainte Madeleine** sugar mill (the largest in the British Empire when it opened in 1870), its ponds and golf course built for staff in 1900. Next is Princes Town, and the road continues to Rio Claro and Mayaro on the east coast. It runs parallel to the south coast, most of which is fairly inaccessible. Near Princes Town is the **Devil's Woodyard**, one of 18 mud volcanoes on Trinidad. This one is considered a holy site by some Hindus (it is also a natural landmark). It last erupted in 1852 and the bubbling mud is cool. There is a series of small mud cones, which often get washed down by heavy rains, not a spectacular volcano. There is a playground and a picnic area.

Waves of immigration – a cosmopolitan nation is born

British rule in Trinidad began in 1797 when an expedition led by Sir Ralph Abercromby captured the island. It was formally ceded to Britain by Spain in 1802 under the Treaty of Amiens. African slaves were imported to work in the sugar fields introduced by the French, until the slave trade was abolished in 1807. After the abolition of slavery, in 1834, labour became scarce and the colonists looked for alternative sources of workers. Several thousands of immigrants from neighbouring islands came in 1834 to 1848, and some Americans from Baltimore and Pennsylvania came in 1841 and Madeiran 'Portuguese' came seeking employment and were joined by small numbers of European immigrants – British, Scots, Irish, French, Germans and Swiss. There was also immigration of free West Africans in the 1840s. In 1844 the British Government gave approval for the import of East Indian labour and the first indentured labourers arrived in 1845. By 1917, when Indian immigration ceased, 141,615 Indians had arrived for an indentured period of five years, and although many returned to India afterwards, the majority settled. The first Chinese arrived in 1849 during a lull in Indian immigration. In 1866 the Chinese Government insisted on a return passage being paid which put an end to Chinese immigration. Labour shortages led to higher wages in Trinidad than in many other islands and from emancipation until the 1960s there was also migration from Barbados, Grenada and St Vincent. Towards the end of the 20th century there was also immigration from Guyana.

South coast → *For listings, see pages 64-82.*

From St Julien, east of Princes Town, a road leads after 19 miles (slow driving) to the fishing village of **Moruga**. Every year around mid-July they have a celebration of Columbus' 1498 landing on the beach. Fishing boats are decked out as caravels, complete with the red Maltese cross. Columbus, a priest and soldiers are met by Amerindians (local boys, mostly of East Indian and African extraction); after the meeting everyone retires to the church compound where the revelry continues late into the night.

The **Karamat mud volcano** at Moruga, erupted in 1997. Thick mud spurted 150 ft into the air, killing one man, burying animals alive and engulfing houses, leaving 100 homeless. Seek local advice before visiting. To get there, from Penal Rock Road proceed west to the eight mile post. On the right head down Haggard Trace driving south until the Moruga West oil field gate. Enter on the road and continue left for one mile. Pass a series of tank batteries, No 7, on the

Amerindian decimation

Trinidad was discovered by Christopher Columbus and he claimed it for Spain on his third voyage in 1498. Whether he named the island after the day of the Holy Trinity, or after a group of three hills that he spied from the sea is a matter of dispute. At that time there were probably seven tribes of Amerindians living on the island. It was their hostility which prevented successful colonization until the end of the 17th century when Catalan Capuchin missionaries arrived. European diseases and the rigours of slavery took their toll on the Amerindian population and by 1824 their numbers had been reduced to 893.

left, and continue to an oil pump on the right. Take the side road for a quarter of a mile. Park near the oil pump at a well-head. Continue uphill. There is another mud volcano at **Piparo**, which erupted suddenly in 1994, destroying a section of the village and cutting off the approach by road from the northeast. What remains is a big expanse of dry mud. Nearby is a large and tasteless house, with adjoining Hindu temple. Now a drug rehabilitation centre, it was once the home of the notorious drug dealer and murderer, Dole Chadee, who was hanged in 1999 along with his associates. The eruption of the volcano was seen by some villagers as divine retribution for Chadee's activities.

The **Trinity Hills Wildlife Sanctuary** lies west of Guayaguayare and was founded in 1934. Its forests are home to a large variety of birds, monkeys, armadillos and opossums. Permits can be obtained from the Wildlife Section of the Forestry Division (T6625114).

It is quite difficult to get beyond Arima and San Fernando by bus, but there are route taxis, and privately operated maxi taxis, or you can hire a car. A full-day circuit of the island can be driven from Port of Spain south to San Fernando, east to Mayaro then north to Sangre Grande and Arima. An alternative route back from Mayaro runs through Biche and the eastern fringe of the Central Range to Sangre Grande.

For hotel and restaurant price codes and other relevant information, see pages 13-17.

⊙ Where to stay

Port of Spain *p33, map p38*

$$$$ Hilton, corner of Lady Young and St Ann's roads, northeast Queen's Park Savannah, T6243211, www. hiltontrinidadhotel.com. Public areas and pool deck are on top and rooms and suites on lower levels down the hillside, facilities for the disabled, restaurants, good catering for special diets, bars, lovely pool, non-residents can eat/swim there (monthly membership), tennis, gym, conference centre, ballroom, executive suite, frequent entertainment. Will arrange taxi from the airport, US$30.

$$$$ Hyatt Regency Trinidad, 1 Wrightson Rd, T6232222, www. trinidad.hyatt.com. Modern waterfront hotel of a high standard, good for business or leisure, contemporary furnishings and all mod cons. Pool overlooking the sea. Very good sushi bar.

$$$$ Kapok, 16-18 Cotton Hill, St Clair, northwest Queen's Park Savannah, T6225765, www.kapok hotel.com. 94 rooms, friendly, comfortable, light, big windows, some studios with kitchenette, excellent **Tiki Village** restaurant with Chinese and Polynesian cuisine, Dim Sum buffet Sun, 1200-1430, also light meals at bar downstairs, small pool, shopping arcade.

$$$$ Radisson Hotel Trinidad, Wrightson Rd, T6253366, www. radisson.com. Formerly the Crowne Plaza. In the business centre, recently refurbished and modern, all facilities very nice, small pool, 2 restaurants, one of which is revolving.

$$$$-$$$ Normandie, off St Ann's Rd, at the end of Nook Av (No 10), T3871242, www.normandiett.com. 54 standard, superior and loft rooms, a/c, reduced rates for businessmen, service criticized, swimming pool, in a complex with craft and fashion shops, and outdoor theatre 'Under the Trees'.

$$$ Cascadia, 67 Ariapita Rd, St Ann's, T6234208, www.cascadiahotel.com. Up in the hills with a great view, nothing within safe walking distance, rooms and suites vary and are in need of renovation, pool with chutes and waterslide not always open and cost extra, tennis and squash courts (Trinidadian national team trains here) and conference facilities, restaurant, bar, poor service.

$$$ Coblentz Inn, 44 Coblentz Av, T6210541, www.coblentzinn.com. Well-run boutique hotel, 17 themed rooms, not all rooms have windows, some fittings need repair, friendly staff, good restaurant with creative international and Caribbean menu, pool some distance away at rental apartment (**Coblentz Cottage**).

$$ Par-May-La's Inn, 53 Picton St, T6282008, www.parmaylas.com. Convenient for Carnival and cricket, double or triple rooms with bathroom, a/c, TV, phone, Wi-Fi, facilities for the disabled, parking, local cuisine

with roti, evening meals on request, credit cards accepted. Nearby the same owner has 15 apartments, **$$ Sun Deck Suites**, 42-44 Picton St, T6229560, www.sundecktrinidad.com. A/c, with cooking facilities, sleep 2/3.
$ Copper Kettle Hotel, 66-68 Edward St, T6254381. Central, simply furnished rooms with shower, a/c, fine for the price, restaurant for breakfast and lunch. Door closed at 1800 for security, ring bell to get in.

Port of Spain suburbs *p41, map p38*

$$$ Allamanda, 61 Carlos St, Woodbrook, T6241480, http:// theallamanda.com. 8 suites, breakfast and Wi-Fi included, friendly, safe, convenient for restaurants and shops and short walk to Queen's Park Savannah, Spanish and Portuguese spoken.
$$$ Courtyard by Marriott Port of Spain, Invaders Bay, Audrey Jeffers Highway, T6275555. 116 rooms and 3 suites, some with auxiliary aids for wheelchair users. Sandwiched between office building and busy highway, overlooks Jean Pierre Stadium. Close to **Movie Towne** complex for shops and entertainment. Designed for business travellers but also conveniently located at Carnival time, desks in rooms, complimentary internet access, TV, parking, pool, fitness centre. **Courtyard Café** for hot breakfast buffet and dinner.
$$$ The Gingerbread House, 8 Carlos St, Woodbrook, T6278170, www.trinidadgingerbreadhouse.com. The prettiest guesthouse in town,

a 1920 traditional house with 3 light and airy guest rooms, a/c, fridge, Wi-Fi, breakfast included, plunge pool, sun deck and garden. Very friendly.
$$$ L'Orchidée, 3 Coblenz Gardens, St Ann's, T6210618, www. trinidadhosthomes.com. A few mins' walk from Queen's Park Savannah, 12 rooms with bathrooms, a/c, ceiling fans, Wi-Fi, excellent breakfast included, other meals can be ordered from local restaurants and served on the patio, exemplary friendly service.
$$$-$$ Alicia's Guesthouse, 7 Coblentz Gardens, St Ann's, T6232802, www.aliciashousetrinidad.com. On a quiet street close to the Prime Minister's residence, 27 rooms, some cheap, all a/c, fan, TV, phone, fridge, family rooms, suites, small pool, jacuzzi, meals available, excursions organized.
$$ La Calypso Guesthouse, 46 French St, Woodbrook, T6224077. Cheaper rooms share bathroom. Some are large with kitchen. Ask to see what's available before choosing one. Good location for restaurants and Carnival.

Western Main Road to Chaguaramas *p43, map p34*

$$$$-$$$ Crew's Inn, Chaguaramas, T6344384, www.crewsinn.com. 46 rooms, ask for one of the refurbished ones, clean and well run, pool, gym, kids' play area, shops, bank, beauty salon and **Lighthouse** restaurant daily 0730-2300 on same marina site, pretty views of the yachts and harbour.
$$$-$$ The Bight, Lot 5, Western Main Road, T6344427, www.peake yachts.com. 10 rooms, simple

accommodation on the waterfront designed for visiting yachties, sports bar, marina, meals daily 0700-2300.

North coast *p46, map p34*

$$$ Laguna Mar Nature Lodge, Blanchisseuse, at milepost 65½ just before suspension bridge over Marianne River, T6692963, www. lagunamar.com. Owned by Fred Zollna, close to beach and lagoon, 2 buildings each with 6 a/c rooms with private bathrooms and a separate 4-bedroom self-catering cottage. Quiet and peaceful, surrounded by forest and birds, no TV, beautiful location with beach and river bathing. **Cocos Hut** restaurant attached, open for food 0700-1900, bar stays open later.

$$$ Maracas Bay Hotel, Maracas, west of beach, T6691914, www. maracasbay.com. 32 a/c rooms with shower and 2 double beds, each with porch overlooking bay. Hotel in need of renovation and repair.

$$$ Monique's Guesthouse, 114-116 Saddle Rd, Maraval, T6283334, www.moniquestrinidad. com, on way to golf course and north coast beaches. Easy access from city, 10 rooms in main house, 10 more over the hill (not advisable if you have mobility problems), large rooms, different sizes sleeping 1-4, a/c, TV, phone, some kitchenettes, **Pink Anthurium** restaurant serves good local food, clean, attractive, facilities for the disabled, staff are helpful and hospitable.

$$$ Second Spring, 13 Damier Village, at milepost 67¾, T6693909, www.secondspringtnt.com. Cottage or 3 studios, breakfast US$10, rustic, comfortable, in gardens on clifftop with wooden walkway, spectacular views of coast, beaches within walking distance, owned by Ginette Holder who is friendly and hospitable, excellent value.

$$$-$$ Zollna House, 12 Ramlogan Terrace, La Seiva, Maraval, T6283731, www.lagunamar.com/zollnahse. htm. Run by Fred and Barbara Zollna in conjunction with Laguna Mar. Comfortable and peaceful, rooms with shared or private bathroom, lovely gardens and good views from hillside.

East of Port of Spain to Arima
p50, map p34

$$$ Airport Inn, Factory Rd, Golden Grove, Piarco, T6698207, www.airport inntrinidad.com. Good bed & breakfast run by Sita Singh, includes transfers to and from airport, Wi-Fi, 4 rooms with bathrooms, clean and comfortable.

$$$ Airport Suites Ltd, 7 Factory Rd, Golden Grove, Piarco, T6690362, www.airportsuitestt.com. 39 rooms with a/c, TV, Wi-Fi, transport to/from airport included, pool, free tea and coffee, restaurant, efficient service.

$$$ Sadila House, Waterpipe Rd, Five Rivers, Arouca, T6403659, www.sadilahouse.com. Run by Savitri and Dinesh Bhola, close to airport, transfers on request. Rooms sleep 1-4 people, credit cards accepted, weekly and group rates available, a/c, TV.

$$$ Xanadu Tropical Resort, Lopinot Rd, Arauca, T6468628, http://xanadutt. com. Good standard of rooms of varying sizes with private bathrooms, a/c, Wi-Fi, breakfast US$11, other meals available, good food and drinks, pool, popular with groups and parties, airport transfers, friendly service.

$$$-$$ Chateau Guillaume, 3 Rawle Circular, Arima, T6676670, http://cguillaumme.caribsurf.net/ joanwilliam@yahoo.com. Run by Matthew and Joan William, 2 double and 2 triple rooms, all with a/c and private bathroom, very clean, lower price for long stay, airport transfers, excellent breakfast, use of kitchen, Wi-Fi, very helpful, Matthew will act as tour guide if needed.

$$$-$$ Pax Guesthouse, Mt St Benedict, Tunapuna, T6624084, www.paxguesthouse.com. Built 1916, the oldest guesthouse on the island, 3 verandas popular with birdwatchers, 147 species of bird on estate, donkey trails into forest, rooms have high ceilings, no a/c necessary, 1 family room, most share showers. The downside is that there is a gap at the top of the doors so the light shines in and you can hear every snore and trip to the toilet in the night. Simple but wholesome food, lovely view of central Trinidad as well as of occasional monk.

North of Arima *p53, map p34*

$$$$ Asa Wright Nature Centre, 7½-mile mark, Blanchisseuse Rd, Arima, T6674655, www.asawright.org. Price includes all meals including afternoon tea, rum punch, tax and service, 2 main-house rooms in colonial style, high ceilings, wooden furniture and floors, fan, bathroom, 24 standard rooms and bungalow in gardens, all designed to be private and secluded, facilities for the disabled, verandas for birdwatching, 80% of guests in high season are birdwatching groups.

$$$ Aripo Cottage, Hollier Trace, Aripo Estate, Heights of Aripo, 9 miles north of Arima, T6626770, http:// aripocottage.wix.com. Cottage in converted cocoa house sleeps 7 in 2 bedrooms, or 3 cabanas sleep 3-6 people, mostly in bunk beds, full kitchens, restaurant, pool, birdwatching, pretty view of mountains, nature trails, river bathing, packages for day visits, also beach apartments to rent at Mayaro Beach.

$$ Alta Vista, up the road from **Asa Wright** heading to Blanchisseuse, T6293262, http://altavistaresorts.com. Set in 16 acres of forest bordering a reserve, 8 basic wooden cabins with bathroom and fan, breakfast US$5, lunch and dinner available or barbecue your own, attractive pool for swimming, veranda overlooking forest, nice waterfall along a trail.

Northeast coast *p55, map p34*
Beach houses in the Toco-Manzanilla area are advertised in the local newspapers. Standards vary, so check first or be prepared for basic standards. Often need to bring own linen, but kitchen utensils usually provided. Places get very booked up during school and public holidays.

$$$$-$$$ Le Grande Almandier, 2 Hosang St, Grand Riviere, T6701013, www.legrandealmandier.com. Also on the beach for turtle watching, good standard of accommodation, a/c, breakfast included, very good restaurant daily 0700-2200, cater to individual tastes including vegetarian, meal plans available, 3 suites sleep up to 6, knowledgeable and accessible proprietor.

$$$ Acajou, 209 Paria Main Rd, Grande Riviere, T6703771, www.acajou trinidad.com. 6 luxurious wooden and bamboo cabanas designed and built by French architect, each with deck overlooking river mouth and beach. One of the nicest places to stay in Trinidad, with delicious food (special diets catered for) and proper coffee served at a very laid-back pace. Parking, Wi-Fi, fishing, snorkelling, tours and transport arranged.

$$$ Mount Plaisir Estate Hotel & Spa, Hosang St, Grand Riviere, T6702217, www.mtplaisir.com. 13 beachfront rooms right by the place where the leatherback turtles nest, nature trails, birdwatching, with excursions organized, overnight camping tours with local guide, restaurant 0800-2100.

$$$ Playa del Este Sanctuary, 13¾ mile post, Toco Main Road, Salybia, T6912632, www.playadel esteresort.com. 40 rooms, standard, deluxe or ocean view, pools and jacuzzis, spa, gym, Wi-Fi, day passes and mid-week special deals including meals, popular weekend getaway, good service.

$$$-$$ McEachnie's Haven, T6701014, http://mytrinidad.org/ Mceachnie.htm. 6 basic but clean rooms, a/c, friendly staff, meals available, use of hotel kitchen. Higher rates for credit cards. On hill opposite the practising hut of local band, **Roots and Branches**, who often perform in the popular bar.

San Fernando *p60, map p34*
$$$$ Cara Suites Pointe-à-Pierre, Southern Main Rd, Claxton Bay, T6592272, www.carahotels.com. 100 comfortable rooms and suites pool, business centre, good Wi-Fi in public areas, cable connection in rooms, bar, view over muddy Gulf of Paria, this West Indian hotel chain is highly regarded. **Metropolitan** restaurant, good creative menu.

$$$ Royal Hotel, 46-54 Royal Rd, T6523924, www.royalhoteltt.com. Designed for business travellers with good rooms and facilities in a lovely hilltop garden with pool. Food and service are good and there is a nice outdoor seating area for breakfast.

$$$ Tradewinds, 36-38 London St, St Joseph Village, San Fernando, T6529463, www.tradewindshotel.com. 41 adequate rooms and suites, some with kitchenette, ask for one away from the noisy club next door, bar, restaurant daily 0500-2300, gym, small pool, jacuzzi, games room.

South coast *p62, map p34*
$$$ Queen's Beach Resort, 187 Gould St, Radix Village, Mayaro, T6305532, www.queensbeachresort. com. Popular weekend getaway on the beach with indoor and outdoor pools. Day passes available. Quieter during the week and sometimes things close. Rooms good although water pressure can be an issue. No sea view except from deck. Ask for exit to beach to be unlocked.

$$$ RASH Resort, Gould St, Mayaro, T6307274, www.rashresort.com. Apartments with full kitchens, family resort, no alcohol in public areas, on the beach, pool, simple accommodation, no restaurant.

$$$-$$ Harry's 4 U, Baywatch Blvd, Grand Lagoon, south end of Mayaro, T7696310, see facebook. Right on beach (plastic litter), nice grounds, rather peculiar building, apartments range in size from tiny room with double bunk bed, kitchenette, bathroom, a/c, TV, to larger units, some with verandas. Busy at weekends, karaoke on Sat.

$ Mrs Paria's, guesthouse, just beyond the BP/Amoco compound, T6308030. Self-contained room, TV, breakfast, beautiful modern home.

---

❶ Restaurants

Port of Spain *p33, map p38*
All the shopping malls have indoor food halls with a varied and good selection of stands selling cheap food of different nationalities during the day, seating in the middle. Some booths stay open until 1800 but supplies become limited after 1330. More elegant and costly dining can be found in the business hotels.

$$-$ D'Bocas, 68 Independence Sq, Brian Lara Promenade, T6273474, www.dbocas.com. Catering for office workers and shoppers, this canteen is good for fish dishes and chicken, with other meats on different days, such as pork or goat, and good Creole vegetables and salads (breadfruit, green bananas, callaloo, sweet potato,

pigeon peas), lunchtimes from 1030, cafeteria-style or take-away. Local fruit juices or *mauby* to wash down the 'belly-full' meals. Fri from 1830 there's live entertainment and DJ.

Port of Spain suburbs *p41, map p38*
Plenty of choice west of city centre: **Ariapita Av** for full price range, from street snack to smart night out. **Maraval Rd** for cheap and cheerful. All along **Western Main Road** in St James there are lots of cafés, snack bars and restaurants, all reasonably priced, lots of choice. Street food is not to be missed as this is where you will get the best doubles, roti and other typically Trini specialities. Generally, the longer the queue, the better the food at the doubles carts. Doubles, costing about TT$5, are fried bara, split-pea dough, filled with spicy chickpeas, mango chutney, *chado beni* (like coriander) sauce and pepper, unless you ask for it without pepper, or 'light' if you don't want too much. Even the cucumbers served with the doubles can have a fiery kick. Part of the fun is watching the skill of the vendor twisting and filling the doubles, particularly if they have a large order which needs to be completed quickly. They can be found in all the busy areas such as Queen's Park or Woodbrook.

$$$ A La Bastille, Ariapita Av and Verteuil St, T6221789, alabastille@ hotmail.com. Mon-Sat breakfast, lunch and dinner. French-run brasserie, good breakfast from 0730 with freshly made croissants, creative menu, good wine, excellent fixed-price lunch.

Roti

A wrapped roti is the lunch of choice for Trinidadians on the go, the hand-held meal and equivalent of the British sandwich. It is also the late-night pit stop, fuel for more partying, much like the ubiquitous kebab or a burrito. It can be filled with split peas, *dhalpuri*, and/or a variety of vegetable and meat curries. The favourite is curried chicken accompanied by curried potato and chickpeas (*channa*), curried mango, pumpkin or other relishes and sauces. Some offer boneless chicken, but Trinidadians generally prefer the flavour of the meat on the bone, sucking and licking clean anything that isn't edible. *Sada* is a plain roti, *dosti* is two-layered and 'buss up shut' is a torn paratha reminiscent of a torn shirt with the curry on the side to dip the bread into.

Everyone has their favourite place to get roti and arguments can break out over each chef's merits regarding the thickness of the roti or the silkiness of the paratha. For some recommendations, see http://trinichow.com or www.macocaribbean.com.

\$\$\$ Aioli, Ellersly Plaza, Bossiere Village, Maraval, T2223291, see facebook. International fare, bistro style with a modern decor yet cosy and intimate. The chef is on hand to talk to customers and service is good.

\$\$\$ Apsara, 13 Queens Park East, T6237659, www.apsaratt.com. Mon-Fri lunch special 1100-1500, Mon-Sat 1800-2300 à la carte. Expensive but mostly good food, pleasant surroundings, North Indian and tandoori rather than Indo-Trini.

\$\$\$ Buzo Osteria Italiana, 6 Warner St, Newtown, T2232896, buzo.trinidad@gmail.com. Italian-owned, real Italian pasta, pizza and desserts. Open kitchen, cheerful chefs. Contemporary design, popular with young professionals, especially for the Fri evening 'lime'.

\$\$\$ Chaud Café & Wine Bar, Damian St, One Woodbrook Place, T6289845, www.chaudcafe.com. Light lunches or café patisserie and snacks followed by wine bar and small plates at night, an eclectic international menu based on Lebanese mezze as much as Spanish tapas, although you can also get a substantial 12-oz ribeye steak and fries. It isn t great for vegetarians but their meat dishes are tasty. Good brunch on Sat 1100-1700. Pleasant deck for outdoor drinking or quiet dining room and bar with world music.

\$\$\$ Hakka, 4 Taylor St, Woodbrook, T6220004, see facebook. Mon-Thu 1100-2300, Fri and Sat 1100-2400, Sun 1200-2200. Fusion Chinese and Indian cuisine with a Trini twist, lots of flavour and spices, good-sized portions, most dishes around US\$10. Dim lighting, red and black colour scheme, indoor and outdoor seating and the advantage of parking space.

$$$ Jaffa at the Oval, 2nd floor, Queen's Park Cricket Club, Tragarete Rd, T6226825. The restaurant is in the pavilion but open to the public. They do a good weekday business lunch buffet with a great choice of desserts, Sun brunch buffet at US$45 per person (children under 12 US$24, under 6 free) and Thu afternoon tea. Good quality, tasty and reasonably priced.

$$$ Tamnak Thai, 13 Queens Park East, T6250647, http://tamnakthaitt.com. Mon-Sat 1800-2300, Mon-Fri, 1100-1500. Thai restaurant although the service doesn't match up to the excellent food, beautiful setting with pretty outdoor area overlooking the Savannah. **Apsara** is upstairs.

$$$ Texas de Brazil, Fiesta Plaza Movietowne Mall, Invaders Bay, T6230022, www.texasdebrazil.com. Lunch Thu-Sun 1100-1500, dinner daily 1700-2230. A US chain of *churrascarias*, this is a carnivore's delight but is also known for the vastness and freshness of the salad bar. The meats can be a bit salty for some tastes, but the service is very attentive and the caipirinhas are excellent.

$$$ Veni Mangé, 67A Ariapita Av, T6244597, www.venimange.com. Mon-Fri 1130-1500, dinner Wed, Fri only 1900-2200. Small, friendly, good home-style Creole food, imaginative menu includes vegetarian dishes. The side dishes accompanying your main course are very good and you can order more if you need. The owner is on hand but the staff don't have service as their main priority.

$$$ Verandah, 10 Rust St, St Clair, T6226287. Mon-Fri lunch 1130-1345, Thu and Sat dinner, 1900-2145. Caribbean ingredients but not just the standard dishes, small menu but good selection, catch of the day is always worth trying. Old house in a pretty location – with a veranda and garden. Family-run, friendly service. There are several other restaurants on Rust St, while round the corner on Maraval Rd you can find Arab, Korean, Chinese restaurants, roti and juice bars.

$$$-$$ Drink! Lounge & Bistro, 63 Rosalino St, Woodbrook, T2237243, see facebook. Open from 1100 until about midnight. Open kitchen, pleasant staff, good food, whether for brunch, lunch, dinner or just drinks, lively atmosphere and a great place to come for a Fri evening 'lime'. They even serve gluten-free pizza.

$$$-$$ Jenny's on the Boulevard, 6 Cipriani Blvd, T6251807. Restaurant Mon-Thu 1100-2200, Fri and Sat 1100-2300. Bar Mon-Thu until 2400, Fri and Sat until 0100. Wide variety of mainly Chinese dishes in elaborate setting, the service can sometimes be awful, in which case you're better with takeaway. Lively pub-style bar downstairs with light meals and snacks, also Chinese. Fri lime starts after work around 1700.

$$$-$$ Peche Patisserie, 45 Picton St, Newtown, T2228508. Tue-Fri 0700-1630, Sat 0830-1530, Sun 0900-1430. The French-trained chef produces authentic French breads, croissants, brioche and fabulous pastries and petit fours. This café is the place to come for breakfast or lunch, offering good coffee and hot chocolate, fresh juices, sandwiches, salads and main courses, often with Trini ingredients, such as saltfish, with a French twist. Breakfast reservations advised at weekends.

$$ Creole Kitchen, 22 Boissiere Village, Maraval, opposite Ellerslie Plaza, next to fuel station, T6229905. Daily 0800-1800. Popular with local workers for lunch, home-cooked Creole food, cafeteria-style, generous portions.

$$ Hott Shoppe, in Maraval Rd and 20 Mucurapo Rd, T6224073. Mon-Sat 1000-2130. Rotis, which are of a slightly heavier texture than some. The skins can be bought frozen to take home. Watch out for the hot sauce.

$$ Irie Bites, 71A Ariapita Av, Woodbrook and 153 Western Main Road, St James, T6227364, www.irie bitesjerk.com. Mon-Thu 1000-2100, Fri 1000-2200, Sat 1000-2100, Ariapita Av location open Sun 1000-1400. Specializes in Jamaican jerk and barbecue meats, combo meals of meat and side bites of your choice, the side dishes can be ordered in larger portions for vegetarians, relaxed atmosphere.

$$ Patraj, 159 Tragarete Rd, T6226219. Mon-Sat 1000-1630. If you are watching cricket at the Oval this is a good place to buy food. Service and quality are patchy though.

Western Main Road to Chaguaramas *p43, map p34*
Popular with yachties, live entertainment some nights.

$$$ Lighthouse at Crew's Inn, T6344384. Daily 0700-2200. Breezy, open on all sides, good view of yachts. Some interesting dishes on the menu, but food can be bland.

$$$ Sails, Power Boats Marina, T6341712. Indoor and outdoor dining on the waterfront, good seafood cooked on the grill. Music some nights. Pleasant service.

$$$ Wheelhouse Pub, 106 Western Main Road, Tropical Marine, T6342339. 1000-2300. Pretty location on the water, cold beer and well-cooked food. Swordfish is good and fresh and on Wed they barbecue it, along with ribs; you get a separate plate for your side dishes, so plenty of food. Sat night is bake-and-shark (and side salad) night, popular with yachties.

North coast *p46, map p34*
$$$ Cocos Hut, also on coast road at Mile 65½ by Marianne River. Small, friendly, usually a choice of fish or meat dishes, slow service but all food freshly cooked. Don't forget the shark-and-bake at Maracas Bay, see Restaurants, page 15.

$$$ Joseph's, Rookery Nook, Maraval, T6225557, www.josephstnt.com. Mon-Fri 1130-1430, Mon-Sat 1830-2230. Arab and other dishes, excellent service, popular, run by a Lebanese, Joe. Inside or outdoor seating.

East of Port of Spain to Arima *p50, map p34*
$$$ Bootleggers, Block F, Trincity Mall, T6408448. Open 1100-2300. Sports bar and grill. Unexciting menu ribs, steaks, Tex Mex, etc but useful if you need somewhere in the east.

$$$ Botticelli's, City of Grand Bazaar, Valsayn, T6458733, www.botticelli-tt. com. Open 1222-2300. Italian and American, pricey but good. Shopping-plaza location, so no parking problems, but restaurant has a very indoors feel.

$$$ Chinese Wok, Trincity Mall, T6403542. Mon-Thu 1100-2100, Fri, Sat 1100-2200. Good and also has branches in **Tunapuna**, T6625296, **Chaguanas**, T6656637, and **Arima**, T6672250.

$$$ Rasam, also at the City of Grand Bazaar, Valsayn, T6450994, www.thenewrasam.com. Mon-Sat 1100-2200. Indian, Chinese (Hakka) and Thai. Sit in a booth for privacy or at tables. Wed Hakka, Fri Thai, Sat Indian buffet nights, 1900-2200, US$35 inc tax and service. Live entertainment Fri and Sat evenings. A/c can be a bit cold.

$$$ Valpark Chinese Restaurant, Valpark Shopping Plaza, Churchill Roosevelt Highway, Curepe, T6624540. Daily (even public holidays) Open 1100-2300. Fairly standard Cantonese menu, but well cooked and well served, unspectacular but pleasant setting, unobtrusive live music some nights. Starters from US$5, main courses from US$8. Buffet dinner Wed, buffet brunch Sun.

$$$-$$ Pax Guesthouse on Mt St Benedict, above Tunapuna, T6624084. Book 24 hrs ahead, enquire about opening times when booking. Very different and slow-paced. Tea is a tradition and all the bread, cakes, jam, honey, etc are handmade by the monks, wholesome and tasty, lovely views of Trinidad from patio. Lunches and dinners available, excellent value.

South of Port of Spain *p58, map p34*

$$$ Bougainvillea, 85 Rivulet Rd, Brechin Castle, Couva, T6364837.

Mon-Sat 1100-2200. Chef claims to specialize in 'American, Italian, Spanish, Creole, Chinese and seafood delights'.

$$$ Buffet King, Centre Pointe Mall, Chaguanas, T6718795. Mon-Thu 1100-1500, 1830-2130, Fri and Sat 1100-1600, 1830-2230. Daily lunch and dinner buffets. Mix of Chinese and non-Chinese dishes, with salad bar and dessert bar. Lunch Mon-Sat US$13, dinner Mon-Thu US$23, Fri and Sat lobster buffet US$29, inc tax.

$$$ Kam-Po, 53 Ramsaran St, Chaguanas, opposite Centre Pointe Mall, T6654558. Mon-Thu 1030-2200, Fri and Sat 1100-2300. A good Chinese restaurant and cocktail lounge. Also has high-quality imported US steaks and seafood.

$$$ Passage to Asia, 7 St Ives St, Chaguanas, T6722701. Unprepossessing exterior on a dingy street, but completely different inside. Wonderful smells greet you as you enter and the service is welcoming. Choose from Indian, Thai or Chinese on the extensive menu.

$$$ Woodford Café, Price Plaza, Chaguanas, T6272233, www.woodford cafe.com. A bit of everything here, from Trinidadian favourites to salads, burgers and pasta. Appetizers with a drink are popular for an evening lime, particularly the saltfish accra with sweet tamarind sauce or the cassava chips. Also at Fiesta Plaza, Movietowne, Invaders Bay, Port of Spain.

San Fernando *p60*

$$$ L'Attitude, 18-24 Quenca St, T6578033, see facebook. One of the best restaurants in town, serving good fresh food, fish straight from the boats daily, vegetarian options, delicious desserts. Good-value lunch specials at US$8-10.

$$$ Palki, 27 Todd St, T6521239. Good Indian food but unreliable service. Lunch special changes daily, good value, usually meat, rice, veggie dish and salad.

$$$ Soongs Great Wall, 97 Circular Rd, T6575050, www.soongsgreat wall.com. Mon-Thu 1100-2200, Fri, Sat 1100-2230. Chinese food, good reputation, the distinctive, Trinidadian version of Chinese food.

ⓝ Bars and clubs

Trinidad has plenty of evening entertainment. For those wishing to visit the places where the local, rather than tourist, population goes, anyone in the street will give directions. The atmosphere will be natural and hospitality generous; it will not be luxurious but the local rum is likely to flow freely. Places run late, starting to get lively around 2300-midnight and closing 0400-ish (any opening hours listed are likely to vary at a moment's notice). Fri has a bigger crowd than Sat but no night is completely quiet. In **central Port of Spain**, clubs and bars tend to be fun but more rough and ready. Several lively bars on and close to Brian Lara Promenade, though some are very dirty. Some of the smarter places are in **Chaguaramas**. All-inclusives are 'free drinks' once you have paid the cover charge, or else free drinks up to a certain time. Less expensive are the 'cooler fêtes',

where you take a cooler with ice and your own drinks. Car parking can be a problem, and there are often traffic jams in and out on the road through Carenage; around **Carnival**, these can last for hours. Other hazards include drivers who have been over-enthusiastic with the free drinks. Closer to Port of Spain, **St James** is famously the 'city that never sleeps'. Further east, in **Tunapuna**, there are several small and lively bars. All along **Eastern Main Road** there are bars and restaurants with a busy crowd, especially on Fri, take your pick.

The centre of **Arima** is full of life in the evenings, especially Fri after work. Lots of little bars, cheap Chinese restaurants, some of which open late. To the south of Port of Spain, the bars in **Chaguanas** are rougher than some but still lively, particularly at weekends to around 0300-0400. **San Fernando** has several clubs worth trying, while **Coffee St** is lively, with plenty of bars.

Port of Spain *p33, map p38*
Club Zen, 9-11 Keate St, close to Queen's Park Savannah, T3514642, see facebook. Wed, Thu, Fri, Sat 2100-0400. Admission depends on the event and whether drinks are 'free', women free some nights. In converted Art Deco cinema, very glitzy, good security, massively floodlit streets around, wonderful views and breeze on roof terrace, but you pay extra for that and VIP area. Easy to run foul of complicated dress codes, rastas with baggy styles not encouraged. Massive queues.
D'Bocas, 68 Independence Sq, T6273474, www.dbocas.com.

A restaurant during the day, see above, but a great place for the Fri night lime, very popular after work. No cover charge. Much the liveliest place in Port of Spain, down to earth, mature crowd.

V&J Brauhaus, 14-17 Ground Floor West Victoria Suites, Victoria Sq, T7750729, www.brauhaustt.com. For beer drinkers, the most extensive selection of European beers in Trinidad. Beer garden, German and eastern European food.

Port of Spain suburbs *p41, map p38*

51 Degrees, 51 Cipriani Blvd, T6270051, www.51degrees.biz. Open Thu-Sat from 2200, closing 'late', dress code varies from night to night, admission fees depend on what you're drinking. Club and radio DJs.

De Nu Pub (Mas Camp Pub), 19-23 Ariapita Av, Woodbrook, T6274042, see facebook. Nightly entertainment including calypso and steel band, best place to see live calypso out of season (cover charge usually US$5); however has managerial ups and downs. Started as Minshall's mas camp in 1980, the Mas Camp Pub was established in 1986, since when calypso shows have been staged every Wed night by the Ward brothers, who have encouraged local music in many forms.

More Vino More Sushi, 23 O'Connor St, Woodbrook, T6228466, and 33 Scott St, San Fernando, T2238466, www.morevino.com. Mon-Wed 1100-2400, Thu-Sat 1100-0100. Very popular wine bar, also sells spirits and cocktails, known for its excellent sushi, sashimi, fine selection of cheeses and hors

d'oeuvres, hookah pipes, indoor and al fresco tables, special set lunch menu US$16.50, after work lime most nights, occasional live DJs and functions, security guards walk you to your car.

Smokey and Bunty, corner of Western Main Road and Dengue St, St James, T6223850. A lively rum shop and sports bar in operation since 1989, usually open until dawn or after at weekends. Most expats and tourists go at least once. It was once open 24 hrs but crime and drugs put a stop to that.

Trotter's, Maraval Rd, T6278768, www.trotters.net. Sun-Thu 1130-2400, Fri and Sat 1130-0200. A local version of an American sports bar, with tacos, pizzas, burgers and steaks, and a British Sun pub lunch menu, but has interesting tabletops decorated with newsclippings of past corruption scandals as well as achievements and success. Reference to trotters is globe, not pigs'.

Western Main Road to Chaguaramas *p43, map p34*

Pier One, Williams Bay, Chaguaramas, T6344518, www.pier1tt.com. Thu-Sat 1200-0400. Smart, hosts many carnival fêtes, lively at weekends, also offers party cruises on board *C/ Prowler*, going around the bay, and private charters.

San Fernando *p60*

HiRPM, Gulf City Mall behind **Burger King**, T2238282. Open until 0400 weekends. Lively, youngish crowd, good mix of music. Karaoke Tue, Pop Rock Wed with live bands and DJs, Boom Box Thu, After Work Lime Fri, Party Sat, DJs and bartenders Sun.

Metro Nightlife, 1014 Gulf View Link Rd, T6576346, see facebook. New in 2013, this multi-million dollar club has a state of the art lighting system to enhance the partying. Bar, dance floor, regular DJ appearances, Thu night Latin night.

⊕ Entertainment

Trinidad *p32, maps p34 and p38*
Casinos
There are several casinos, some of which run through the night. They are small and seedy by Bahamian or Aruban standards, but you can lose money just as effectively: slot machines, blackjack, roulette, etc, with 'free' sandwiches to keep you at it and 'free' drinks if you lose heavily. Well known are **Ma Pau**, in Ariapita Av and **Island Club**, at Grand Bazaar shopping mall, open pretty much round the clock. Alternatively you can lose money in smaller amounts in most bars and neighbourhood shops through government-run gambling: *Play Whe*, which is based on traditional Chinese gambling, and the weekly *Lotto* draw.

Cinemas
See listings in daily papers.
Caribbean Cinemas 8, Trincity Mall, near highway to Piarco, T6407473, www.caribbeancinemas.com/trincity. A multiscreen.
Movie Towne, on highway west of Port of Spain, T6278277, www.movie towne.com. US-style 10-screen Cineplex surrounded by shops, restaurants, bars and other entertainment. General admission US$8, 3D more expensive, matinees cheaper.

Theatres
See press for details of performances.
Central Bank Auditorium, Eric Williams Plaza, Edward St, Port of Spain, T6230845.
Little Carib, White and Roberts sts, Port of Spain, T6224644, see facebook.
Naparima Bowl, 19-21 Paradise Pasture, San Fernando, T6522526, is the centre for performing arts in the south.
Queen's Hall, 1-3 St Ann's Rd, Port of Spain, T6241284, http://queenshalltt.com.

○ Shopping

Trinidad *p32, maps p34 and p38*
Most shops take US dollars and credit cards at around TT$6=US$1. The main **Port of Spain** shopping areas with arcades are **Frederick St**, **Queen St**, **Henry St** and **Charlotte St** (fruit and vegetables). In San Fernando there are arcades on High St and in central Trinidad arcades line Chaguanas Main Road. However, Trinidadians do most of their shopping in malls (www. trinidadmalls.com), of which there are several large new complexes with food halls and entertainment centres as well as supermarkets, clothes shops and household goods. Of international standard with mostly imported goods, they charge international prices. The main shopping centres are **Movie Towne Entertainment Complex**, Invader's Bay, Port of Spain; **The Falls at West Mall**, Westmoorings; **Long**

Circular Mall, St James; **Ellerslie Plaza**, Maraval; **Trincity Mall**, Trincity; **The City of Grand Bazaar and Valpark Shopping Centre** in Valsayn; **Cross Crossing Shopping Plaza** at Lady Hailes Av, **San Fernando and Gulf City Shopping Complex** in La Romain are also popular.

Purchases can be made at in-bond shops in Port of Spain and at the airport. There is a huge selection of duty-free shops.

Arts and crafts
Bargains can be found in fabrics, carvings, leather and ceramics. Souvenirs include mini steel pans, sandals, belts, ornaments, jewellery, packs of dried seasonings and cocktail mixes, soaps and lotions. Handicrafts can be purchased at some markets and beach vendors will offer you bracelets, necklaces and pendants. In Port of Spain there are street vendors on **Frederick St**, **Independence Sq** and elsewhere selling hand-painted T-shirts, etc. Crafts can be found at **East Mall** on Charlotte St and at the cruise ship complex. Batik can be bought at many places in most malls and at **Rainy Days**, at Ellerslie Plaza, Maraval.

Food
Locally grown fruit and veg is often heavily sprayed, so wash well or peel. Markets offer a wide variety of fruit and veg. **San Juan** opens from about 0400, lively, good selection, also bars and eateries which make a last stop when everywhere else has closed as Fri night turns into Sat morning. The **Central Market** at Sea Lots is the largest market, cheap fruit and veg, opens very early, but there are also sizeable markets in San Fernando, Chaguanas, Princes Town, Arima and Sangre Grande. Best to visit any market early, from 0600-1100. Fresh fish by **Western Main Road** in Carenage or on the highway near Valsayn.

Music
Crosby's Music Centre, 54 Western Main Road, St James, or **Kam's**, Long Circular Mall, St James. Production costs are a problem so prices of local CDs are high, and despite being the main music outlets in this island of music they frequently have no stock. Bootlegged copies are, however, sold widely in downtown Port of Spain.

○ What to do

Trinidad *p32, maps p34 and p38*
Cricket
Cricket is very popular. Test matches are played at **Queen's Park Oval**, T6222295, the oldest ground in the Caribbean, west of Queen's Park Savannah, Port of Spain, renovated for the 2007 Cricket World Cup; take a cushion, sunhat/umbrella, whistle (!) and drinks if sitting in the cheap seats. It is a private club but a friendly gate guard might let you in for a look around when matches are not being played and if you ask politely. There are smaller grounds for club cricket throughout both islands. For information on regional and international matches, see www.windiescricket.com.

Diving

Underwater visibility is not as good as around Tobago because of the silt washed around the island by the outflow of the Orinoco River. However, the nutrients in the current attract huge manta rays, whale sharks and other large pelagics so, if you can see, there is lots to see. Most diving is off the Chaguaramas Peninsula and the Bocas islands, where it is more protected and the water is clearer, with some interesting underwater formations. **Dive TnT**, at Coral Cove Marina, Western Main Road, T6342872, www.divetnt.com/divetrinidad, has all-day dive trips most weekends from 0900 in either Trinidad or Tobago. There is also **Rick's Dive World**, Tardieu Marine, Western Main Road, T6343483, www.ricksdiveworld.com.

Fishing

The seasons for sport fishing in Trinidad are sailfish: Nov-Apr; kingfish, African pompano and Spanish mackerel: Jun-Sep; dolphin fish and wahoo: Oct-May; tarpon, tuna, shark and other species can be fished all year round. Most offshore fishing takes place along the north coast and in the Gulf of Paria, while tarpon fishing is good off the Bocas islands. Charters can be arranged, for deep-sea fish or bonefish and tarpon in the mangroves and flats. Prices for deep-sea fishing are around US$500-600 per day from the marinas in Chaguaramas for a fully equipped charter boat, but you can negotiate lesser fees with private fishermen. The annual **Wahoo Tournament** is held in Mar,

International Marlin Madness in Apr, the **Kingfish Tournament** in Jun and a **International Trinidad Tarpon Thunder Tournament** in Aug. Contact the **Trinidad and Tobago Game Fishing Association**, T6326608, www.ttgfa.com for information.

Football

There are many football stadiums on Trinidad. The Hasely Crawford and Marvin Lee stadiums are home to Trinidad's national football team: Pro League matches (Apr-Dec) are played there and at the Larry Gomes (Arima), Ato Boldon (Couva) and Manny Ramjohn (Marabella) stadiums. Others around the island include the Queen's Park Oval (shared with other sports), Arima Municipal Stadium, Dwight Yorke Stadium in Bacolet, and Guaracara Park, Pointe-a-Pierre. Many players from Trinidad and Tobago play for top football clubs in Europe and the USA, including Carlos Edwards and Kenwyne Jones who play for British clubs. Dwight Yorke is one of the best known of Trinidadian footballers, playing for many years for Manchester United, where he became one of the top 10 highest goal scorers in the Premier League, before moving to Australia in 2005. He captained the Trinidad and Tobago team in the 2006 World Cup in Germany, the smallest country ever to qualify for the finals. Football fever has since gripped the nation and members of the 'Soca Warriors' team (www.socawarriors.net) are national superstars. The team failed to progress far enough through the qualifying rounds for the 2010 and 2014 World Cup finals in South Africa and Brazil. There is also a national women's team, the Soca Princesses, professional and secondary school leagues, and clubs for children. **Trinidad & Tobago Football Federation (TTFF)**, T6237312, www.ttffonline.com; T&T Pro League, T6454489, www.ttproleague.com.

Golf

There are 6 golf courses on Trinidad. The loveliest is the 18-hole Championship **St Andrews (Moka) Golf Course**, Moka, Maraval, T6294653, which has a popular clubhouse, bar, restaurant and pool. Another challenging course is the 18-hole Championship PGA-designed **Millennium Lakes** par 71 course at the Country Club at Sunrise Park Trincity, close to the airport. There is another 18-hole, USGA-rated par 70 course at the Petrotrin **Pointe-a-Pierre Golf Club** outside San Fernando. Also in the San Fernando area is the par 34, 9-hole course at the **Usine Ste Madeleine**, a former sugar estate and mill. The course was built around 1900 on undulating land and each fairway slopes. Former sugar cane fields have also been used to create the **Brechin Castle** 9-hole golf course in Couva, which has small greens and undulating land. The best of the small golf courses is probably the **Chaguaramas** par 67, 5646-yard course with its 9 holes and 18 tee boxes on former cocoa plantation land. Built by American servicemen stationed there during the Second World War, it has some glorious trees and bamboo and is close to Edith Falls and Macqueripe Bay.

Horse racing

There is horse racing at **Santa Rosa Park**, Arima, about 9 miles outside Port of Spain, www.arimaraceclub.com. Built in 1982, the complex has an administrative building, exercise track, stables, a viewing gallery, a car park, quarantine area and a children's playground. Races are held here most Sats and public holidays.

Horse racing in Trinidad dates from 1828 when informal races were held at Queen's Park Savannah, known as the Big Yard, and other locations including beaches. 1897 saw the establishment of the Trinidad Turf Club (replaced in 1976 by the Trinidad and Tobago Racing Authority) and the construction of the race stand on the Savannah, acknowledging the popularity of the sport and the competitiveness of the owners, trainers, jockeys and horses. Rebuilt in 1947 the stand was also used for cricket, football and golf audiences as well as for ceremonial parades and Carnival.

Kayaking

Sea kayaking (including tuition) can be arranged through the **Kayak Centre**, Western Main Road, Williams Bay, Chaguaramas, T6337871, run by Merryl See Tai, 500 m after the Alcoa dock, just before Pier One.

River kayaking is best in the rainy season when there is more water in the rivers. Eric Blackman, T6693995, takes guided tours up the

Marianne River on the north coast, see page 49. **Caribbean Discovery Tours**, T6247281, runs kayak tours into the to the Bush Bush Sanctuary in the Nariva Swamp, no previous experience necessary and a great way to see the wetland.

Sailing

Chaguaramas is the main area for sailing and racing, with lots of marinas catering for local and foreign yachts. **Trinidad and Tobago Sailing Association (TTSA)**, T6344210, www.ttsailing.org, sponsors **Carnival Fun Race** and a weekly racing programme in winter and spring when the winds are at their strongest. It also runs a sailing academy with sailing courses and sailing camps for newcomers. Every Jul/Aug, there is a power boat race from the **Trinidad and Tobago Yacht Club (TTYC)**, Trinidad to Store Bay, Tobago.

Squash

Cascadia Hotel, Ariapita Rd, St Ann's, T6233511, has 2 courts with seating for 100 spectators per court, tennis courts, sauna and gym with lots of equipment and facilities, open for non-members but difficult to get a booking, Mon-Fri 0600-2100, Sat 0900-1700.

Surfing

The best swells can be found off the north and northeast coasts in Nov-Mar, although hurricane season can also provide some spectacular waves. Some of the best beaches include Sans Souci, Las Cuevas, L'Anse Mitan, Grande Riviere, Roughside and Salybia. There are several national and international competitions throughout the year, contact the **Surfing Association of Trinidad and Tobago (SATT)**, see facebook.

Tennis

Tennis Association of Trinidad and Tobago, www.tennistt.info, has a list of tennis clubs on Trinidad and Tobago. Some hotels have tennis courts for use of guests which can sometimes be used by others for a fee, such as the **Hilton** and the **Cascadia**, but courts are not common.

Tour operators

Avifauna Tours, Ahie Villa, Sierra Leone Rd, Diego Martin, T6335614, www.rogernecklesphotography.com. Tailor-made, high-end eco-tours with wildlife photographer and naturalist Roger Neckles.

Banwari Experience Ltd, River Rd, Bourg Mulatresse, Lower Santa Cruz, T6215893, banwari@tstt.net.tt, run by Andrew Welch, offers cultural and nature tours, hiking, birdwatching, Carnival.

Caribbean Discovery Tours Ltd, 9B Fondes Amandes Rd, St Ann's, T6247281, www.caribbeandiscovery tours.com, run by Stephen Broadbridge. Walking tours, cave exploration, kayaking expeditions, good trips to Nariva Swamp, and other trips off the beaten track. Camping (in basic-luxury tents or cabins) or lodging in guesthouses arranged for longer trips, tailor-made tours.

Pier One, T6344472, www.pier1tt.com. Offers all-inclusive tours for 3 hrs around the offshore islands or all day to Chacachacare, 1000-1600, good for large groups, you rent the boat with drinks, food, security, etc. The boat can also be rented for evening cruises with DJ, bouncers and bar packages, when there is a dress code. **Trinidad and Tobago Sightseeing Tours**, 165A Western Main Road, St James, T6281051, www.trintours.com. Speak German, Italian, Spanish and French, will arrange accommodation and car hire, evening tours, sightseeing tours, deep-sea fishing, naturalist tours, panyard visits, tickets for carnival fêtes, etc.

◎ Transport

Trinidad *p32, maps p34 and p38*
Air
Flying is the most time efficient way of travelling between the islands. See Air, page 10, for details of flights between Trinidad and Tobago.

Boat
See Transport in Trinidad and Tobago, page 10, for the ferry between Trinidad and Tobago. Drug dealers and pirates operate in these waters so behave with extreme caution. Small boats are likely to be intercepted by Venezuelan or Trinidad coastguards, or both.

Bus
PTSC office (T6232341) is located at South Quay railway station, called City Gate, and is the main terminal for both buses and maxi taxis, the hub for public transport. One-way fares range from TT$2-12, fares within Port of Spain are TT$2.50. A/c buses, **Express Commuter Service** (ECS), with an a/c lounge for waiting passengers, run on the main routes from City Gate Terminal to **Arima**, **Chaguanas**, **Five Rivers**, **Sangre Grande**, **Chaguaramas** and **San Fernando**, also from **Arima** to **Sangre Grande**. They are usually every hour on weekdays but less frequent at weekends. Rural buses are extremely infrequent and unreliable.

Maxi taxis have fixed routes identified by the coloured bands on the sides of the vehicles: yellow (Route 1) for the west of Trinidad including **Chaguaramas**, **Petit Valley** and **Diego Martin**, departing from a fenced compound at the corner of St Vincent St and South Quay, Port of Spain; red (Route 2) for the east to **Sangre Grande** from City Gate, South Quay; green for **Curepe** and **Chaguanas** and down to **San Fernando**; black from San Fernando along the south to **Princes Town**; brown from San Fernando to the southwest including **Point Fortin**, **Cedros** and **Siparia**. They follow set routes but have no timetable although they don't run after about 2100. Fares start from TT$3. Port of Spain to **San Fernando** is TT$15, the same as the ferry, which is quicker. **Unified Maxi Taxi Association** is T6243505. See also page 12.

Car
The speed limit is 80 kph/50 mph on highways and 55 kph/34 mph in built up areas. The major international car rental companies such as **Avis**,

Budget and National are all represented. Local companies include Singh's Auto Rentals Co Ltd, www.singhs.com, Kalloo's Auto Rentals, www.kalloos.com and Southern Sales & Service Co Ltd in San Fernando, www.southernsalestt.com. Many companies have offices at the airport. See also page 12.

Taxi

Check airport taxi fares at the tourist information offices, T6695196 at Piarco International and T6390509 at ANR Robinson International, where current fares are displayed.

Trinidad *p32, maps p34 and p38*
A lot of places, eg University of the West Indies, are listed under 'T' for 'The' in the phone book. **Medical services** There are hospitals in Port of Spain and San Fernando, as well as several district hospitals and community health centres. **Port of Spain General Hospital**, 169 Charlotte St, T6232951. **Mount Hope**, T6454673, has better facilities. **St Clair Medical Centre**, T6281451, is private, more comfortable, expensive, but not necessarily better equipped. **West Shore Medical**, 239 Western Main Road, Cocorite, T6229878, is new, well-equipped and expensive.

Contents

Footprint features

Tobago

Tobago is not as busy and vibrant as Trinidad but the island is charming, beautiful and ideal for people in search of relaxation. Trinidadians regard it as their holiday island. The tourist area is low key and concentrated on the southwest end, about six miles from the capital, Scarborough. There are small hotels and guesthouses scattered all around the island, however, offering peace and quiet in beautiful surroundings. The forest on the central hills is quite wild and provides a spectacular backdrop for the many horseshoe bays around the coast and there is good walking, birdwatching and diving. Tobago is 26 miles long and only nine miles wide, about the same size as Barbados, but with only a fifth of the population and a tiny fraction of the number of tourists. It is shaped like a cigar with a central 18-mile ridge of hills in the north (the Main Ridge, highest point 1890 ft), running parallel with the coast. These northeast hills are of volcanic origin and the southwest is flat or undulating and coralline. The population is concentrated in the west part of the island around Scarborough. The majority are descended from African slaves and there is not such a diverse mix of races as on Trinidad. The climate is generally cooler and drier, particularly in the southwest, than most parts of Trinidad.

Arriving in Tobago → *Country code: 868.*

Getting there
There is a good ferry service and air shuttle to Scarborough from Trinidad, while many international flights come direct to Tobago.

Getting around
Many hotels are within walking distance of the airport and close to the beach. Scarborough is only 15-25 minutes' drive from Crown Point Airport and small enough to walk around, but for trips to the suburbs or further afield take a route taxi or hire a car. If you are driving around Tobago, some of the minor roads are suitable only for 4WD. If you are hiking, get the three 1:25,000 sheets, not currently available in Tobago but obtainable from the Lands and Survey Division, Richmond Street, Port of Spain, or from a good map shop. It is possible to walk anywhere. There is a book of trails.

Tourist information
There are tourist offices at the airport and at the port with printed information and maps available.

Scarborough → *For listings, see pages 99-115.*

Scarborough is the capital of Tobago and the centre of all business activity on the island. Boats come into the bay bringing cargo and passengers and there is a lively market at the water's edge, best on Fridays and Saturdays, with a fair degree of traffic congestion. A seafront promenade has been developed with stalls selling food and souvenirs along the walkway heading west from the port. The town is pleasant but perhaps not worth an extended visit. There are very few places to stay or eat as tourist development has been concentrated elsewhere.

Places in Scarborough
In Scarborough itself the **Botanic Gardens** ⓘ *Claude Noel Highway, T6757034*, on the hill behind the mall are worth a visit. Dating from 1899, they cover 10 acres of hillside, showcasing mostly native plants but also some African and South East Asian imports. Entrances are off the Claude Noel Highway and from Gardenside Street.

There are also some interesting structures, such as the **House of Assembly** ⓘ *www.tha.gov.tt*, on James Park. It was built in 1825 when it housed the island's legislature and judiciary but representative government was abolished in 1877 when the island became a Crown Colony. **Gun Bridge**, Bacolet Street, is interesting too with its musket-barrel railings and cannon at either end, relocated from Fort King George when the bridge was widened in the 1950s. What was the Governor's House on Mount William, built in 1828 and used by governors of the twin-island colony when on Tobago, is now the official residence of the President of the independent nation.

New development has included a deep-water **harbour** and **cruise ship terminal**. **Scarborough Mall** is modern, concrete and rather tatty but most activity is around here, including the market, where you can find local varieties of fruit and vegetables, clothing, meat and fresh coconut water. Away from

Tobago

Where to stay 📍	Blue Waters Inn **1**	Conrado Beach Resort **15**
Ade's Domicile **22**	Candles in the Wind **11**	Crown Point Beach **15**
Adventure Eco-Villas **10**	Castara Cottage	Footprints Eco Resort **16**
Angel Apartments **13**	Apartments **13**	Gloucester Place
Arnos Vale Vacation	Changrela Cocrico Inn **17**	Guest House **18**
Apartments **12**	Charlotteville Shark	Hummingbird **15**
Bacolet Beach Club **8**	Shacks **14**	Johnston Apartments **15**
Blue Haven **25**	Cholson's Chalet **14**	Kariwak Village **5**
Blue Mango **13**	Coco Reef **2**	Lesville's Place **19**

the market, the main shopping area is the **NIB Mall**, which has souvenir and craft shops as well as clothes and household retailers. The **Central Library** is a modern building dating from 1982. **St Andrew's Anglican Church** on Bacolet Street was built on the foundations of the original church completed in 1819 but blown away by Hurricane Flora in 1963. There are banks on Main Street and Carrington Street.

Above the town is **Fort King George** ⓘ *T6393970, Mon-Fri 0900-1700, TT$5/US$0.80*, which is well maintained and has good views along the coast. You must drive through the hospital to get to the fort. Building commenced in 1777 and continued under the French in 1786. Fort Castries was renamed Fort Liberté in 1790 after the garrison revolted, recaptured by the British in 1793, returned to France in 1801 and, after the island was ceded to Britain in 1802, named Fort King George in 1804. It was decommissioned in 1854. The gardens are attractive and well kept and there are excellent views over Scarborough. There are a number of historic buildings here including the Officers' Mess, the Barrack Guard House, the Magazine (almost hidden under an enormous silk cotton tree), the Bell Tank (still with water in it and an amazing echo), and a lighthouse to guide ships around the reef into Scarborough harbour. A number of cannon mounted on metal garrison gun carriages can also be seen. There are two of the late artist Luise Kimme's huge wooden figures in the middle of the parade ground which are very attractive. At the Officers' Mess, the **Tobago Museum** has an excellent small display of early Tobago history including Amerindian pottery, military relics, maps and documents from the slave era. Beautifully restored in 2006, the yellow ballast bricks look almost as

good as new. The layout and structural design of the renovated buildings has been preserved as it was prior to the hurricane of 1847.

East from Scarborough → *For listings, see pages 99-115.*

Off the coastal road you can go to the **Forest Reserve** by taking a bus from Scarborough to **Mount St George** and then walking or hitching to **Hillsborough Dam**. The lake is the drinking-water supply for the island so swimming is not allowed. It is a lovely forest setting. A 4WD vehicle is necessary if you want to drive but the walk there is recommended. From there continue northeast through the forest to **Castara** or west to **Mason Hall** on an unpaved, rough road. A guide is not necessary, as there is only one path. Birdwatching is excellent (oropendulas, motmots, jacamans, herons) and there are cayman in the lake, but look out for snakes (none of them poisonous). Alternatively, take a taxi to Mason Hall (ask the taxi to drop you at the road for the Hillsborough Dam) and walk to Mount St George via Hillsborough Dam, which is easier walking as the track is on the level or downhill, about nine miles.

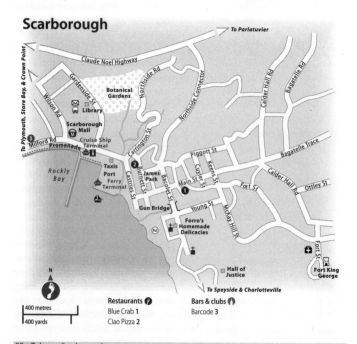

Scarborough

Restaurants 🍽	Bars & clubs 🍸
Blue Crab **1**	Barcode **3**
Ciao Pizza **2**	

Colonial Tobago

Tobago is thought to have been discovered by Columbus in 1498, when it was occupied by Caribs. In 1641 James, Duke of Courland (in Latvia), obtained a grant of the island from Charles I and in 1642 a number of Courlanders settled on the north side. In 1658 the Courlanders were overpowered by the Dutch, who remained in possession of the island until 1662. In this year Cornelius Lampsius procured Letters Patent from Louis XIV creating him the Baron of Tobago under the Crown of France. After being occupied for short periods by the Dutch and the French, Tobago was ceded by France to Britain in 1763 under the Treaty of Paris. But it was not until 1802, after further invasions by the French and subsequent recapture by the British, that it was finally ceded to Britain, becoming a Crown Colony in 1877 and in 1888 being amalgamated politically with Trinidad. By some reckonings Tobago changed hands as many as 29 times and for this reason there are a large number of forts. Trinidad and Tobago were granted independence as a twin-island state in 1962 and Tobago has had internal autonomy since 1987, although it is still heavily dependent on its larger sister.

By Mount St George, Tobago's first, short-lived principal town, then called George Town, is **Studley Park House** and **Fort Granby**, which overlooks Barbados Bay. There isn't much left of the fort, which once guarded George Town. You can see the grave of an unknown soldier and admire the view from the windswept promontory and the park where there is some play equipment for children; a good picnic spot.

The coastal road continues through **Pembroke** and **Belle Garden** ⓘ *www.bellegardenwetland.org*. In recent years, Belle Garden has received UNDP funding to clean up and preserve the local riverine wetlands between the village and the coast, and also to train tour guides for the area. There is a range of birdlife and other fauna and flora is increasing, partly due to a five-year hunting ban. See website for information on tours. There is also an art and craft shop and you can opt for tasting heritage cuisine.

Nearby is **Richmond Great House**, a beautiful plantation house built in 1766, now used as a guesthouse. It is full of antiques and memorabilia of the days of slavery collected by the owner, Professor Lynch, and has a glorious hilltop location with views of the ocean. Having started out as a sugar plantation, after the collapse of the industry at the end of the 19th century new owners diversified into cocoa and coconuts. The passage of Hurricane Flora in 1963 destroyed the plants but the house survived, along with a few immortelle trees

The legacy of Dr Eric Williams

The first political organizations in Trinidad and Tobago developed in the 1880s, but in the 1930s economic depression spurred the formation of labour movements. Full adult suffrage was introduced in 1946 and political parties began to develop. In 1956, the People's National Movement (PNM) was founded by the hugely influential Dr Eric Williams, who dominated local politics until his death in 1981. The party won control of the new Legislative Council, under the new constitutional arrangements which provided for self-government, and Dr Williams became the first Chief Minister. In 1958, Trinidad and Tobago became a member of the new Federation of the West Indies, but after the withdrawal of Jamaica, in 1961, the colony, unwilling to support the poorer members of the Federation, sought the same Independence rights for Trinidad and Tobago. The country became an independent member of the Commonwealth on 31 August 1962, and became a republic within the Commonwealth on 1 August 1976. Dr Williams remained Prime Minister until his death in 1981, his party drawing on the support of the ethnically African elements of the population, while the opposition parties were supported mainly by the ethnic Indians.

which stand as a reminder of the cocoa trees they used to shade. The house and 4 acres were bought by Tobagonian Professor Lynch in 1973 and over the years he has carefully restored and preserved it. Other surviving old plantation houses on the island include Kings Bay House at Kings Bay, Kendal House at Kendal and Yeates House at Milford Bay.

Roxborough, the island's second town, also on the Windward coast, is worth a visit. The **Argyll River waterfalls** ⓘ *T6604154, www.argyllwaterfall. org, 0900-1700, TT$40/US$6.60 for foreign adults, children half price*, near Roxborough, are a 10-minute walk upstream from the road and easily accessible. There are four beautiful falls with a big green pool at the bottom where you can swim. The attraction is run by a local co-operative: guides are available, included in the entry fee for foreigners, not really necessary as the path is obvious, but they can be most informative. The agile can scramble up the path from the bottom pool to the higher levels and pools and then the top of the falls. Part of the Main Ridge Forest Reserve, the falls are a good introduction to the rainforest, with a wide variety of trees and flowering plants attracting a wealth of birds and butterflies. There are toilets and a gift stall selling cocoa balls, jewellery and trinkets.

Tobago Cocoa Estate ⓘ *Cameron Canal Rd, Roxborough, T7883971, www. tobagococoa.com, estate tours US$10, 1 hr, Mon, Wed, Fri 1100 or at other times by appointment*, is a lovely old cocoa estate, renovated by Tobagonian Duane

Dove, a sommelier, after he acquired the hilly, overgrown land in 2004. Various tours are offered, showing the way cacao is grown, harvested, fermented, dried and made into cocoa. Cocoa beans from this estate are made into award-winning, single-estate chocolate by artisan chocolatier, François Pralus, in France. Rum and chocolate tasting is offered in some tour packages also involving breakfast, afternoon tea or dinner. Visitors are shown the principles of companion planting, using plants such as cassava and plantain which offer temporary shade to the young cocoa trees and can be sold for additional income. Cassava is also made into bread in the enormous traditional brick oven built for the purpose. Tradition is key at this Heritage Park and Dove has built a drying house out of Trinidadian cedar so that the prime cocoa beans never touch metal or concrete, for a better flavour.

For a good walk take the road from Roxborough to Parlatuvier and Bloody Bay through the **Main Ridge Forest Reserve**. This is the oldest protected forest in the Western Hemisphere, dating from the 1760s when it was realized that the island's water supply could not be guaranteed if the forest was cut down. You go through singing forests with masses of birds including cocricos, collared trogon, motmots, jacamans and hummingbirds. After the five-mile marker is a semi-circular trail in the forest called **Gilpin's Trace**. There are great views from the hut at the top of the road. This is the place people are usually brought on birdwatching tours as the guides know in which trees to find particular birds, the route is not taxing and there is a wide variety of plants and insects to see. There are several other walks in the forest and guides have their own favourites, where they know where to find particular birds.

Beyond Roxborough is **King's Bay**, with waterfalls near the road in which you can swim. They are only a five-minute walk from the main road along a paved track, so very accessible. They are best in the rainy season when the extra water makes the falls more dramatic. King's Bay itself is a sheltered cove despite being on the Atlantic, or Windward, coast, and is quite good for swimming. Changing facilities are available.

Speyside and Little Tobago → For listings, see pages 99-115.

Speyside

The fishing village of Speyside is set on a broad bay with islets offshore and a backdrop of forested hills. There are places to stay and eat here and it is a good base for snorkelling, diving and birdwatching excursions. The **Speyside Waterwheel** is a relic of the island's sugar plantation days. Scottish-made and erected in the late 18th century, it powered the sugar cane grinding machinery for nearly 100 years until the collapse of the industry at the end of the 19th century.

Tobago's beaches

Tobago is noted for its beaches, two of the best being only minutes from the airport: **Store Bay**, popular with locals, lots of vendors, food stalls and glass-bottom boats; and **Pigeon Point**, a picture-postcard beach fringed with palms with calm, shallow water protected by **Buccoo Reef**. You have to pay to use the facilities at the beach, but you get changing space, umbrellas and beach bars. Here also there are lots of glass-bottom boats going out to Buccoo Reef and a catamaran for coastal tours and swimming in the Nylon Pool, a shallow area offshore. Other good beaches on the leeward side of the island are **Stone Haven Bay**, **Mount Irvine Bay** and **Courland Bay**, one of the longest. All have resort hotels and watersports. **Castara** is a pretty bay cut in two by rocks jutting out into the sea. The forest comes down to the water at either end and a river can be followed from the sea up to some waterfalls. **Englishman's Bay** is another lovely bay, with the forest coming down to the beach and a river running into the sea. The east coast is more rugged and windswept. **Hillsborough Bay**, just outside Scarborough, has a glorious beach, but the sea is dangerous because of rip tides. Do not swim there. **Big Bacolet Bay**, also known as Minister Bay, is great for surfing, body surfing and boogie boarding, but watch out for the currents. **Bacolet Bay**, by the Blue Haven Hotel, is a better bet for swimming as it is protected by rocks and a reef. In the northeast, **King's Bay** has a beach bar, toilets and huts for shade. There is a signpost to the beach, almost opposite the track to **King's Bay Waterfall**. **Speyside** and **Charlotteville** both have protected bays. From the former you can take glass-bottom boat trips to **Little Tobago** with birdwatching, walking and snorkelling included and from the latter you can walk to Pirate's Bay through the forest. Snorkelling is good on the reef here.

Little Tobago

A lovely trip is to this forested islet off the northeast coast, a sanctuary for birdlife. There are wild fowl and 58 species of other birds, including boobies, birds of paradise, motmots and, most spectacularly, the red-billed tropic bird found here in the largest nesting colony in the north Atlantic. Boats across cost US$25 (includes a guided tour of the islet and snorkelling). There are lots of glass-bottomed boats which leave from **Blue Waters** Inn and boatmen will find you fish and coral to see. Go early in the morning if you are a keen birdwatcher, but the afternoon tours are still rewarding. If you want to camp, you are supposed to have prior permission from the **Forestry Division** ⓘ *Studley Park, T6394468*. They also have a rudimentary

Tobago's protected areas

On Tobago, apart from two reserves (Buccoo Reef and the virgin and secondary forests of east Tobago), there are the **Goldsborough** natural landmark, the **Kilgwyn** wetland, which it is hoped will be designated a scientific reserve, the **Grafton** nature conservation area, the **Parlatuvier–Roxborough** scenic landscape, and three recreation parks (including Mount Irvine). The Main Ridge Rainforest is the oldest rainforest reserve in the Western Hemisphere but has not yet been made a national park. At the **Grafton Bird Sanctuary** some of the world's most beautiful birds,

the blue crowned motmots, are fed at 0800 and 1600 at the Old Copra House. They are not tame enough to be hand-fed but it is still a spectacular sight. Many of the small islands (Saut d'Eau, Kronstadt Island and Soldado Rock off Trinidad, and Little Tobago, St Giles and Marble Islands off Tobago) are reserves for wildlife with the largest seabird colonies in the southern Caribbean. They are important breeding grounds for red-billed tropic birds, frigate birds, man-o-war and other seabirds. A permit is needed to visit these areas, usually arranged through a tour guide.

camp on main ridge by the Roxborough–Parlatuvier road, which can be used by arrangement.

Pigeon Peak

From Speyside you can climb Pigeon Peak, at about 1900 ft it is the highest point on the island. There are two routes up the hill through the forest, the shorter one is steeper than the longer one, so both take about three hours. There is also a track on the Speyside Road from Charlotteville, 300 ft on the right before the turning to Flagstaff Hill. This is suitable for a 4WD to begin with. After about 30 minutes' walk you clamber down into a stream bed and up again, from which point it becomes a rough, steep path through old banana plantations and then woodland. There is no trouble following the path here, with markers cut into or painted on to trees, and there are many birds. However, when the ground becomes flatter, it becomes confusing. A guide is therefore essential. The actual summit is above the woodland, through grass and small shrubs, and has a trig point. From the top you can see the north and south coasts and offshore islets.

A trip to Charlotteville in the northeast is recommended. There are magnificent views on the way and the village itself is on a fine horseshoe bay with a good beach, lifeguard, good swimming and snorkelling and dive shops. The easiest way to get there is by one of the seven buses a day from Scarborough (US$1.28). There are also maxi taxis from Scarborough (US$1.60, three a day but not on Saturday, when the Adventist drivers do not work; for the return journey you can arrange to be picked up).

Flagstaff Hill

During the Second World War the Americans erected a radio tracking station on Flagstaff Hill overlooking Charlotteville (take the rough track off the main Speyside–Charlotteville road about half a mile). There are several seats and a bandstand here so you can sit and admire the view looking out over **St Giles Islands** and the most northerly tip of Tobago. Sunsets are spectacular here. These islands and rocks, also known as the Melvills, were presented to the government in 1968 by the owner of the Charlotteville Estate, to be preserved as a wildlife sanctuary. They are now one of the most important breeding grounds for seabirds in the southwest Caribbean, including noddy terns, brown boobies, red-footed boobies, red-billed tropic birds and frigate birds.

Pirate's Bay and Man O'War Bay

Halfway along the rough road to Flagstaff Hill there is a cattle path to the right. Follow this as it descends and curves to the left. Near the bottom it meets another, wider trace (trail). Turn left and this will eventually bring you back to Charlotteville. It is a pleasant, shaded walk. From Charlotteville, it is a 15-minute walk uphill, from where you get glorious views of the pristine crescent below you and over the green ridge of mountains, then down 156 steps to **Pirate's Bay**, which is magnificent and unspoilt and good for snorkelling. Being on the north coast, however, it can sometimes be affected by strong waves. Do not attempt to drive along the rough track; park in Charlotteville and walk. There are no facilities, so take any food and drink you might need and bring back your rubbish. Also adjacent is **Man O'War Bay**, which got its name from being a safe anchorage for fighting ships in the 18th century. It is a beautiful bay and has quite good swimming.

Campbellton Bay

Campbellton Bay is a 30- to 40-minute walk from Charlotteville (ask for directions) through dense forest to a secluded beach, mostly used only by fishermen. Campbellton Battery was built to protect shipping when traders came to collect sugar. Two guns were installed here in 1777, along with others elsewhere on the coast, during the American War of Independence, to deter American privateers.

North coast → *For listings, see pages 99-115.*

Charlotteville to L'Anse Fourmi

The road between Charlotteville and L'Anse Fourmi along the Caribbean coast is partly paved and passable in dry weather with 4WD but is not recommended. However, it is a wonderful hike. The views are worth the trouble, with lots of lovely bays beneath you. It is a comfortable four-hour walk along the track from **Charlotteville** to **L'Anse Fourmi** via **Man O'War Bay**, **Hermitage** (bush rum for sale) and **Corvo Point**. The terrain is undulating, bird life is plentiful, including parrots, and you may see iguanas. Take water with you.

L'Anse Fourmi to Castara

The stretch of road between **L'Anse Fourmi** and **Moriah** through the picturesque fishing villages of **Parlatuvier** and Castara is smooth, traffic is light and the views are very scenic, taking in lovely bays, sandy beaches and rocky headlands, cloaked in forest and ringing to the sound of birdsong. The road across the island from Roxborough through the Forest Reserve joins the north coast road at Bloody Bay, just east of Parlatuvier. This is the road used by public transport, which is limited at the best of times. There is no public transport between Parlatuvier and Plymouth along the north coast. Between Parlatuvier and Castara is **Englishman's Bay**, a perfect horseshoe-shaped bay with forest tumbling down the hillsides to the sand and a river running out to the sea: one of the prettiest beaches on Tobago. You are likely to have the place to yourself, particularly mid-week.

Castara

The small fishing village of Castara on the coast is a pleasant place to visit or stay. The bay is hemmed in by cliffs and forest, but contains two sandy beaches separated by rocks, **Big Bay** and **Little Bay**, also known as Heavenly Bay, and a snorkelling reef. Apartments and guesthouses are perched on the hillside above Little Bay, while restaurants are dotted along the beaches. A small river comes out at Big Bay, and a 10-minute walk inland will take you to an easily accessible waterfall. Lifeguards are on duty daily at Big Bay at the Castara Beach Facility.

Local women produce excellent bread and bakeries every Thursday from a traditional clay oven behind the beach at Big Bay. Watch them mixing, kneading and leaving the dough to prove on banana leaves, before baking. The Fisherman's Fete is held here in August, an enthusiastic party on the beach.

Crown Point to Mount Irvine Bay

At the southwest end of the island there are many hotels and resorts, particularly in the **Crown Point** area. At **Store Bay** stand the ruins of small **Milford Fort**, and brown pelicans frequent the beautiful but crowded beach, which is a good place to watch the sunset. The fort was once Dutch (Bella Vista) but was overrun by the Indians. The British maintained a small battery here from 1770-1781 when the French took over the island, and a small fort from 1811-1854 but it is now no more than a nice garden. **Store Bay Beach Facility** ⓘ *daily 1000-1730, lockers, changing rooms, toilets, beach chairs for rent,* has a large car park and stalls for vendors of T-shirts, beach wraps and souvenirs as well as a food court for snacks, local specialities such as crab and dumpling, curry goat, ice cream and drinks. Vending is not allowed on the beach. Boat trips go out from here to the **Nylon Pool** and **Buccoo Reef** for snorkelling. There is some hassling to sign up to excursions and single women have complained of harassment on the beach.

Pigeon Point ⓘ *T6390601, entry fee TT$15/US$2.50, children US$0.50,* has the island's most beautiful beach, clean and with calm water. There are huts, tables and benches, lockers, bars, shopping, boat hire and watersports. It is another good place to watch the sunset. There is no snorkelling from the shore, but snorkelling trips are available and you can take a glass bottomed boat out to Buccoo Reef and the Nylon Pool, US$15.

Mount Irvine Bay is split by a headland, with Old Grange Beach on one side and Little Irvine, or Mount Irvine Beach on the other. Like Pigeon Point beach, the water is good for swimming and the sea is usually calm, but on rougher days there is good surfing. There are beach facilities with changing rooms and cabanas. At the Mount Irvine Bay Hotel, where there is an attractive, palm-fringed championship golf course, you can see the remains of an old sugar mill, now incorporated into the hotel bar and restaurant. The mill was part of the Old Grange Estate and was built at the end of the 18th century, functioning for about 100 years until the sugar industry collapsed.

From Mount Irvine you can walk up to **Bethel** (about two miles), the island's highest village, for excellent views across the island. Another beach well worth a visit is **Turtle Bay**.

Black Rock and around

Northeast along the coast you come to Black Rock, near where are the ruins of **Fort Bennett**. This lookout point offers a panoramic view of the coastline, an advantage when the fort was first built by the Courlanders in 1680 and later when batteries of cannon were positioned there by the British in the 18th century to deter American privateers.

Buccoo Reef

Glass-bottomed boats for visiting this undersea garden leave from Pigeon Point, Store Bay and Buccoo Bay. The charge is about US$15 for two to 2½ hours, with snorkel provided; wear a hat. Longer trips with barbecue cost around US$50-60, worth it if you eat and drink plenty. The dragging of anchors and greed of divers as well as temperature changes resulting in bleaching of the coral have tarnished the glory of this once marvellous reef (you may prefer to make the trip to Speyside where glass-bottomed boats make trips over a pristine reef). Elkhorn and other corals have been badly damaged by snorkellers and divers walking on them, but there is still a good variety of fish, including reef sharks and the colourful parrot fish and angel fish, while shoals of squid can be seen. The reef is protected by law; it is forbidden to remove or destroy the corals or other marine life. Boat trips also include the **Nylon Pool**, an emerald-green pool in the Caribbean. Boats leave between 0900 and 1430, depending on the tide. Be selective in choosing which boat – and captain – you take for the trip; some are less than satisfactory.

Also near Black Rock is the **Grafton Caledonia Wildlife Sanctuary** ⓘ *feeding time 0800, 1600, free*, established on a former cocoa estate. Now seriously in decline, the former Copra House Restaurant was once the drying house for coconut and cocoa and, if you come at feeding time, you can watch the blue crowned motmots and other birds emerge from the forest to be fed, a tradition that has continued since 1963, when the owner started to feed the wild birds after Hurricane Flora destroyed their woodland habitat. There are nature trails through the forest for walkers and birdwatchers. The lack of information and the generally unkempt nature of the place means that it is best to arrange a specialist guide before visiting if you want to understand the place fully. Mr Sampson, who feeds the birds, is knowledgeable and can offer information, but he is not a guide.

Plymouth

The main town on this coast is Plymouth, with **Fort James** overlooking **Great Courland Bay** (site of the Courlander settlement in the 17th century). Named after Jacobus (James), the Duke of Courland, it was destroyed and rebuilt several times as a battery and fort, but is the oldest fort site in Tobago. The present fort was erected in the early 19th century. Also here is the Couronian (Latvian) Monument. Designed by a local artist, it was erected in 1976 during a cultural visit by Courlanders in exile and represents 'Freedom'. A much-quoted attraction in Plymouth is the enigmatic tombstone of Betty Stevens (25 November 1783), which reads: "She was a mother without knowing it, and a wife, without letting her husband know, except by her kind indulgences to him." Plymouth is the site of an international jazz festival held on the sports field by Fort James which attracts many famous artistes. There is also a heritage festival in the summer.

Around Arnos Vale

Hidden in the forest some miles from **Arnos Vale** is the **Arnos Vale Sugarmill**, dating from 1880, where quite a lot of the old plantation machinery can be seen, including the waterwheel which powered the mill. **Arnos Vale Waterwheel Park** ① *T6600815*, has a restaurant and stage where shows are put on. Just off the Arnos Vale Road is the 12-acre **Adventure Farm and Nature Reserve** ① *T6392839, www.adventure-ecovillas.com, Mon-Fri 0700-1745, US$10*, where you can stroll among fruit trees, picking mangoes and other fruit in season while looking for birds, butterflies, iguanas and other wildlife. The owners feed the birds and some 40 species have been attracted to the organic farm, including five of the six hummingbird species on Tobago. These can be easily photographed while you sit on the veranda eating home made soursop ice cream. There are cottages to rent in this relaxing spot, perfect for birdwatchers who want to rise at dawn. The family's very friendly Labrador dogs are in charge of 'meet and greet'.

⊚ Tobago listings

For hotel and restaurant price codes and other relevant information, see pages 13-17.

◉ Where to stay

Scarborough *p85, map p88*

$$$$ Bacolet Beach Club, 73 Bacolet St, T6392357, www.bacoletbeach club.com. This small, quiet hotel has a variety of rooms of different sizes but all have a balcony and lovely sea view. Steep steps down to secluded beach and bar. Service can be friendly and helpful or indifferent. Food nothing special and you need to be down early for the breakfast buffet before it runs out.

$$$$ Blue Haven, Bacolet Point, T6607400, www.bluehavenhotel.com. Lovely location, excellent service but not posh. Built in 1940s, its heyday was in the 1950s when movie stars like Robert Mitchum, Debra Kerr, Jack Lemmon and Rita Hayworth stayed here while making *Fire Down Below*, *Heaven Knows Mr Allison*, or *Swiss Family Robinson*. The original building perched on the point has been restored and new wings with flying roofs have been built either side, one overlooking pretty Bacolet Beach and the other looking out to Scarborough and the Atlantic. All 51 rooms have a sea view, balcony and are light and bright. Some rooms have a window between the bathroom and bedroom so you can watch the sunset from your tub. Eco-friendly policies for water, waste management, energy and food, local natural products in bathroom.

Beach bar for lunch, restaurant up the hill for breakfast and dinner, wonderful food, glorious view.

$$$ Oasis Guesthouse, Signal Hill, T3570317, see facebook. 13 rooms and studios, some with kitchenette, modern and pristine in a quiet area, a/c, good Wi-Fi, pool, jacuzzi, car hire can be arranged.

$$$-$$ Ade's Domicile, 19 Old Lighthouse Rd, Bacolet Point, T6394306, www.adesdomicil.de. Quiet, residential area, short walk to 3 beaches, sea view. 2 studios downstairs, a/c, fan, large room, good kitchen, all very spacious, TV, veranda with furniture under cover, 2 1-bedroom apartments upstairs, also roomy with balcony and better view. Owner, Ade, lives in house above with her dogs.

East from Scarborough *p88, map p86*

$$$ Richmond Great House, Belle Garden, T6604467. Quiet and peaceful hilltop location for this beautiful 1766 plantation house stuffed full of antiques and with a glorious sea view. The housekeeper can prepare delicious meals for you, or you can use the kitchen. Facilities include a pool and tennis court.

Speyside and Little Tobago *p91, map p86*

$$$$ Blue Waters Inn, Batteaux Bay, Speyside, T6604341, www. bluewatersinn.com. An isolated and delightfully unsophisticated hotel,

38 large a/c rooms and efficiencies, some interconnecting, with sea view, and 3 bungalows at the other end of the property with 1 or 2 bedrooms, caters for people who want to sit on the beach, hikers, birdwatchers and divers, also wheelchair accessible. Rate includes tax and service. Dive packages with **Aquamarine Dive** on site, tennis, games room with TV, library, table tennis. Very pretty bay, no other development, view of Little Tobago, great swimming, snorkelling and diving, but food is expensive and service comes without a smile.

$$$$ Nabucco's Resort Speyside Inn, Windward Rd, Speyside, T6604852, www.speysideinn.com. Managed by **Extra Divers Worldwide**, 18 rooms, 3 cabins, 3 bungalows, lovely airy rooms, nicely furnished, small beach across road, pool, dive shop, view of Little Tobago, restaurant with good food but terrible service, also close to **Jemma's** restaurant.

$$$ Manta Lodge, Windward Rd, Speyside, T6605268, www.manta lodge.com. A popular dive lodge, simple but friendly, with good service and great diving. 22 adequate rooms, small pool, friendly bar, restaurant with good food, dive and tour packages available with **Tobago Dive Experience** on site.

$$$-$$ Top Ranking Hill View Guesthouse, Top Hill St, Speyside, T6604904, http://toprankingtobago. com. 5 rooms and suites of different sizes sleeping 2-4 people, with kitchenettes, balcony or patio and view, run by Ann and Max Davidson. 10-min walk down to beach and restaurants, quite a climb back up. The expert birdwatching guide, Newton George (see Birdwatching, below), lives next door and you can visit his hummingbird gallery. Max operates one of the glass-bottom boats at **Blue Waters Inn**.

Charlotteville *p94, map p86*
Lots of basic places to stay, just turn up and look around, advance reservations are difficult to arrange. However, everywhere will be full at festival times.
$$$ Charlotteville Shark Shacks, Northside Rd, Campbleton Bay, T7676420, www.shark-shacks.com. Next to **Man O'War Bay Cottages**, there are 2 rooms attached to the dive shop run by Caroline, 1 double, 1 twin, both self-catering with kitchenette, en suite bathroom and terrace, Wi-Fi and a/c available at extra charge.
$$$ Cholson Chalets, 72-74 Bay St, contact Pat Nicholson (T6398553). Across the road from the dark golden beach where fishing boats come in, looking towards Campbleton Bay with Pirate's Bay to the right. Old family residence with great grandmother's wooden house in the garden; 1 apartment has the matrimonial bed the family was born in. 6 apartments, vary in size and character but all are green and white, spotlessly clean, bright white linens, with partition walls allowing air circulation in the roof but little privacy. Lots of rules for safety and conservation of resources. Herbs, fruits and aloe vera in the garden for guests' use. Very popular and you may need to book in advance even

in low season; advance bookings of less than a week are not accepted.

$$$-$$ Man O'War Bay Cottages, T6604327, www.man-o-warbay cottages.com. 10 cottages in a range of sizes, good for groups with lots of single beds, spacious, right on safe beach with tropical gardens behind, rustic setting, barbecue facilities. Great location with good swimming and beach but only basic accommodation and Charlotteville's shops are not well-supplied with provisions.

$$$-$$ Ocean View Apartment, 11 Mission Rd, T6604891, www.ocean view-tobago.com. 3 apartments with kitchen, a/c, TV, on the hillside overlooking the bay, lovely sunset watching from the veranda. Simple but clean and tidy. Run by Mr Dillon, who is helpful and informative.

North coast *p95, map p86*

$$$ Blue Mango, 2 Bay Rd, Castara, T7680007, www.blue-mango.com. Owned by friendly Colin Ramdeholl, traditional wooden cottages and apartments sleep 2-4, with kitchen, bathroom and fan, mosquito nets, balconies and hammocks, Wi-Fi, charming, built on cliffside between the 2 beaches, rustic but lovely location and views, good walking and swimming, the **Clay Kitchen** restaurant is on site. No credit cards, no extra taxes or service charges.

$$$ Castara Cottage Apartments, T7571044, www.castaracottage.com. 3 apartments on 2 floors sleep up to 10 if all booked together. Upstairs are a studio and a 2-bedroom apartment which interconnect and downstairs

there is another 2-bedroom apartment. A sofabed is available for extra accommodation. Set on the point between the 2 beaches a bit like a treehouse, the apartments have lovely views and get plenty of breeze through the huge windows. Good kitchens, hammocks, simply furnished.

$$$ Gloucester Place Guesthouse and Villa, Parlatuvier, www.gloucester place.com. 3 rooms in the guesthouse, open Nov-Apr, and 2 bedrooms available in **Essex Cottage**, open all year. On a hillside just outside the village with a river running one side of the property with waterfall and swimming hole, the house and cottage are in lovely gardens full of fruit trees which attract lots of birds, with an infinity pool and wonderful views over the sea. Owners Bea and Win are most hospitable and provide a wonderful breakfast with other meals on request.

$$$-$$ Angel Apartments, Heavenly Bay, Castara, T44-1787-282671 (UK), www.angel-apartments.com. 4 dark a/c apartments on ground floor opening on to pool, 8 apartments on middle and upper floors with balcony and sea view, price higher for top floor, which is quieter. Close to beach and restaurants.

$$$-$$ The Naturalist Beach Resort, Castara Bay Rd, Castara, T6395901, www.naturalist-tobago.com. 14 varied but spacious and comfortable apartments for couples or families, car hire can be included, right on the beach with lovely balconies and verandas, internet café, helpful and friendly service.

The southwest *p96, map p86*

There are lots of guesthouses and small hotels along the road between the airport and Pigeon Point, all within walking distance of the airport. Heading east along the coast there are several all-inclusives or package holiday hotels, such as the **Grafton Beach Resort** and its upmarket sister hotel, **Le Gran Courlan** at Stonehaven Bay, Black Rock, or the older Turtle Beach, run by **Rex Resorts**, where 95% of the guests are British.

$$$$ Coco Reef, eastern end of Store Bay, T6398571, www.cocoreef.com. Modelled on a Bermudan hotel, peach and white walls, red roof, 135 rooms, suites and villas on man-made beach with calm lagoon for good swimming, set in 10 acres of manicured gardens and lawns, pretty view of Pigeon Point, a bit frayed around the edges but still comfortable, close to airport and in main hotel area with nightlife in walking distance. Spa and gym for workouts and relaxation.

$$$$ Kariwak Village, Store Bay Local Rd, Crown Point, T6398442, www.kariwak.com. A little oasis in main tourist area 5 mins' walk from airport and Store Bay Beach and the nicest place to stay in this area. Allan and Cynthia Clovis started the hotel in the 1970s, concentrating on guests' physical and spiritual well-being. Beautiful and aromatic gardens with flowers, fruits, herbs and vegetables, lots of birds and butterflies, hammocks and jacuzzi. Morning stretch, yoga, tai chi and other activities most days, free for guests, occasional yoga retreats with international instructors. Thai yoga massage, Shiatsu massage, aromatherapy, hot stones, biophoton light therapy and other treatments to promote healing and regeneration. 18 simple but comfortable rooms around main pool, 6 more in gardens. Open-air thatched restaurant serves excellent, fresh and wholesome food, with menus changed daily, vegetarian options, Tobagonian specialities for breakfast, lunch and dinner.

$$$$ Magdalena Grand Beach and Golf Resort, Tobago Plantations Estate, T6608800, www.magdalenagrand.com. If you want a resort hotel, this is the best on the island. All 200 rooms and suites have a sea view. Part of a 750-acre development around Petit Trou Lagoon, with hotel, villas, condominiums bungalows, championship Jack Nicklaus golf course. On a very windy bit of coast, the hotel is plagued with rust from the salty breeze, but the rooms are comfortable and well equipped, the pools are good although there always seems to be a shortage of towels, and the food is good, particularly breakfast. Very remote, you need a car/taxi to go anywhere; daily shuttle to Pigeon Point where the sea isn't so rough, watersports centre at both locations.

$$$$ The Palms Villa Resort, Signal Hill Old Rd, Signal Hill, T6351010. www.thepalmstobago.com. 5 villas in gated community with security. Pretty colonial-style architecture with large central gardens and play area on hilltop above Scarborough. Each villa has good-sized pool with children's section, barbecue and outdoor eating area, sleep up to 6 adults, comfortable bedrooms, lots of storage space, car hire useful, 10 mins to beach.

$$$$-$$$ Footprints Eco Resort, Culloden Bay, T6600416, http://footprintsecoresort.com. Set in 62 acres of nature reserve, 2 villas, 1 honeymoon retreat, 2 suites and 8 seafront rooms, all on stilts and made from recycled or waste timber, well equipped, palm roofs, solar powered with a/c, great views over sea, saltwater pools at low tide, good snorkelling on reef, quiet and peaceful except for very noisy cocrico birds at dawn calling across the valley. **Cocoa House** restaurant has retreating roof, serves seafood and healthy meals. Get to it from Golden Lane, which passes the enormous silk cotton tree that is supposed to be the grave of Gan' Gan' Sarah. Airport and port transfers included.

$$$$-$$$ Viola's Place, Birchwood Triangle, 101 Hampden Rd, T6399441, www.violasplaceapthotel.com. 10 studios, 4 1-bedroom apartments, 6 with 2 bedrooms, on 2 floors, kitchenette, basic equipment, pool, restaurant, good-sized rooms but no windows. Right by golf course Tobago Plantations, just over a mile to beach.

$$$ Adventure Eco-Villas, Adventure Farm & Nature Reserve, Arnos Vale Rd, Plymouth, T6392839, www.adventure-ecovillas.com. 2 delightful wooden cottages on stilts looking out over the forest with a shared deck, ideal for birdwatching, or a smaller, darker, cheaper apartment attached to the main building. The cottages have a double and single bed, bathroom with

tub, living/dining area with louvre windows which can be opened up completely, well-equipped kitchen, cheerful, painted blue and yellow, surrounded by lush green vegetation, forest noises and birdsong. Popular with families. Beach and shops in walking distance.

$$$ Conrado Beach Resort, Milford Extension Rd, between Store Bay and Pigeon Point, T6390145, www.conradotobago.com. Breakfast included, beachfront, standard or superior rooms, some small, some with balconies, some roadside view, not fancy but priced accordingly, a/c, Wi-Fi, restaurant on beach for breakfast, inside for night-time, good snorkelling offshore on small reef, fishing boats moored outside so better to go to Pigeon Point for beach, family-owned, excellent service.

$$$ Crown Point Beach Hotel, T6398781, www.crownpointbeachhotel.com. Prime position on cliffs at end of Store Bay looking down onto beach and in walking distance (even with luggage) from the airport. Studios, 1-bedroom apartments and cabins, all with sea view, basic self-catering, pool, pleasant grounds, tennis, table tennis, Wi-Fi, mediocre restaurant and pleasant outdoor bar with friendly staff.

$$$ Johnston Apartments, Crown Point, T6398915, www.johnstonapartments.com. Guests have use of **Crown Point** pool, restaurant and tennis court. Spacious, 1-3 bedroom apartments scattered over clifftop garden, steps to beach, short walk to airport, good location.

$$$ Native Abode, 13 Fourth St, Gaskin Bay Rd, Bon Accord, Crown Point, T6311285, www.nativeabode. com. Modern, comfortable house in pretty gardens with fruit trees and plenty of birds. Very hospitable owners of this B&B go out of their way to accommodate guests' wishes and the breakfast is superb.

$$$-$$ Arnos Vale Vacation Apartments, Arnos Vale Rd, Plymouth, T6391362, www.arnosvaleapartments. com. Run by hospitable, helpful Victor Forde, very spacious 1- or 2-bedroom apartments, huge open plan kitchen and living area, fully furnished and comfortable, upstairs apartment has balcony overlooking beautiful garden with fruit trees and tropical birds which come to the feeders, transport to airport, car hire available and a good idea. Excellent value, very popular.

$$$-$$ Changrela Cocrico Inn, Commissioner and North streets, Plymouth, T6392961, www.changrela. com. 1970s concrete block-style inn with rooms and apartments on 2 floors, some with self-catering facilities. Simple accommodation but about the cheapest in the area. Parking, pool, restaurant and bar, Wi-Fi. Owners live on site.

$$$-$$ Hummingbird, 128 Store Bay Local Rd, Crown Point, T6350241, www. hummingbirdtobago.com. Pleasant small hotel and restaurant for breakfast and evening meal. Rooms are on 2 floors around a pool, most of them on the ground floor. Good service, Wi-Fi, a/c, 2 suites have kitchenettes, knowledgeable and experienced Anglo-Trini hosts, Paul and Linda Mountjoy.

$$$-$$ Lesville's Place, Canaan Feeder Rd, Canaan, T6390629, www. tobagolesville.com. Run by Lestell and Orville Moore, who live alongside this new block of rooms, studios and apartments in a quiet residential area off the beaten track. Simple accommodation, large rooms with small bathrooms and kitchens, TV, a/c or fan, tiled floors, no smoking, one of the few properties on Tobago with solar-powered hot water, fruit trees all round with produce for guests, car hire, transfers, beach trips, public transport close by. Popular with Trinidadian tourists.

$$$-$$ Moonlight Mountain Retreat, off road to Plymouth, T6394346, www.moonlight-mountain.com. Perched up in the hills above Scarborough, with views to both the Caribbean and Atlantic and breezes from both oceans. Traditional but modern house with balconies and wooden fretwork set in lush gardens and forest, used for yoga retreats or just B&B. 4 bedrooms upstairs, one with en suite, the others share 2 bathrooms, self-catering apartment downstairs, simple yet stylish furnishings. Plunge pool, hammocks, very relaxing, run by Ginny (yoga teacher) Plumpton and Kelly (great cook) Almann, who also know all the best places to lime, where bands are playing and where to dance. Massage and reflexology available. Local and international breakfast and evening meal by prior reservation. Meals served buffet style on the veranda, delicious smoothies with fruit from the garden.

$$ Candles in the Wind, 145 Anthony Charles Crescent, Bon Accord, T7655335, www.candlesinthewind. 8k.com. Hostel-style with 8 rooms on 2 floors and a kitchen on each floor, also attic dorm with 12 beds, **$** per person. Quiet, welcoming, convenient, with restaurants and beach in walking distance.

🍴 Restaurants

Scarborough *p85, map p88*

In out-of-the-way areas there is often no phone signal and therefore credit cards may not be accepted. Take plenty of cash when you go out for a meal, just in case.

$$$ Basil's, 133 Shirvan Rd, T4702486. Tue-Sun 1100-late. Friendly service and delicious Creole food, good fish and seafood.

$$$ The Blue Crab, corner of Main St with Fort St, T6392737, www.tobago bluecrab.com/bluecrab.html. Mon-Fri 1100-1500, Mon, Wed, Fri evenings by reservation. Specializes in local seafood, very good lunch, dinner is a set menu with a choice of fish, lots of fresh veg, reasonable prices, nice view over harbour. Alison and Kenneth often do all the cooking and serving themselves in the evening, so don't be in a hurry.

$$$ Ciao Pizza, 20 Burnett St, T6352323, see facebook. Wed-Mon 1145-1445, 1800-2200, dinner only on Sun. Italian owned, authentic home-made pizzas cooked in a wood-fired oven, with wide range of toppings, also pastas and salads. Reservations advised.

$$$ Salsa Kitchen Tapas Restaurant, 8 Pump Mill Rd, T6391522. Tue-Sun 1800-2300. Small and intimate. Tapas Tobago-style, home-made pizzas and a dish of the day. Food cooked fresh to order so be prepared to sit over a rum punch or two. Well worth the wait or pre-order. Reservations essential.

$$-$ Rena 'Chatack' Roti Shop, Old Milford Rd, T6357684. A great roti shop serving all sorts of curried meats. There are a few tables but most locals get their lunchtime roti to take away.

East from Scarborough *p88, map p86*

$$$-$$ King's Bay Café, Windward Rd, Delaford, King's Bay, T7712716, see facebook. Mon-Tue 1200-1800, Fri and Sat 1200-2000, Sun 1200-1700. Looks like a simple roadside house, but walk through and you get to a veranda with wonderful view of the bay, a perfect location to eat some of the best food on the island. Known for its excellent burgers and brownies but the grilled catch of the day should not be missed. Everything is fresh and delicious, the fish caught in the bay below and the tuna burgers superb.

Speyside and Little Tobago *p91, map p86*

$$$ Bird Watcher, Windward Rd, Speyside. Lunch and dinner. Casual village restaurant with limited and simple menu but serving wonderful fish, shrimp and lobster from US$25, depending on weight. Chicken and vegetarian options also available. Good place to come after a morning's dive or while touring the island.

$$$ Jemma's Sea View, Speyside, T6604066. Sun-Thu 0800-2100, Fri 0800-1600, closed Sat. Originally a platform on stilts above the beach, now expanded into a large restaurant but still with good view to Goat Island and Little Tobago. Good, filling lunch or dinner, slow service, nice atmosphere but suffers from being on the tourist trail, no alcohol.

Charlotteville *p94, map p86*
$$$-$$ Gail's, on seafront as you walk to Pirate's Bay. Breakfast and dinner from 1900 but they close early if there are few guests, no lunch. All fresh, very tasty, delicious vegetables and salad, Gail is a genius with fish, very friendly.
$$$-$$ Sharon and Phebe's, T6605717. Mon-Sat 0900-2300, Sun 1100-2300. Nice view of the bay from upstairs, very good and cheap meals, try the prawns if available, dumplings and curried crab also good, very friendly, Phebe also has a laundry and special prices for people on yachts.

North coast *p95, map p86*
$$$ The Boat House, Heavenly Bay, Castara, T4830964. Sun-Fri for breakfast, lunch and candlelit dinner. Colourful decor, with fabric strips hanging from the ceiling all over the restaurant. Casual beach bar serving local food but a bit upmarket, very good when owner Sharon is on site, staff slacken in her absence. Drummers and limbo Wed night, sometimes steel pan, when reservations are needed because it is so popular and there is a charge.

$$$-$$ Castara Retreats, Castara, T7661010, www.castararetreats.com/restaurant.htm. Café Wed-Sun from 1030, restaurant daily from 1800. Lovely view overlooking the bay with hummingbirds visiting the feeders and great sunset watching. Run by a Venezuelan/Trini couple, the food here is a notch above most other places. Excellent handmade pasta and the fish and vegetarian dishes are very tasty. Leave room for dessert, when they use local cocoa and coconut in their creations. Also very good for light bites and fresh fruit drinks during the day.
$$$-$$ D'Almond Tree, Castara, T6833593, frasermariska@gmail.com. Lunch and dinner. Excellent service from owner Mariska at this beachside restaurant. Fresh fish daily from local fishermen, lamb also good. No alcohol licence but you can take your own or try the fresh juices. Renovated 2014 with extra tables and colourful floor.
$$$-$ The Coffee Shop (Cheno's), Main St, Castara. Good place to come for breakfast, whether you want bacon and eggs or local saltfish and coconut bake, or to stop by for home-made ice cream. Very friendly and popular. Also known for Sat night entertainment with steel pan, US$16 for barbecue and music, which can start late.

The southwest *p96, map p86*
$$$ Café Coco, beside **Coco Reef Hotel**, off Pigeon Point Rd, T6390996. Pleasant setting with lots of tiles on the walls, fairy lights and plants and fishponds. Open kitchen serves up fusion cuisine, from Cuban and Jamaican to Tobagonian and even

Thai dishes, tasty, fresh, well presented. Service is sometimes exemplary, sometimes non-existent.

$$$ The Fish Pot, Pleasant Prospect, Grafton Rd, Black Rock, T6351728, fishpot.tobago@gmail.com. Tasty fresh fish with a variety of accompaniments, pleasant service and atmosphere for lunch or dinner.

$$$ Food4U, Old Store Bay Rd, Bon Accord, T4863141, dfood4u@gmail.com. Al fresco dining in simple surroundings but the food is elegantly presented, a picture on every plate. Owner Derrick serves local food such as callaloo and crab and dumplings or fresh fish, shrimp, pork and chicken, with tasty morsels of local specialities to garnish the dish. Service can be slow if the restaurant is busy as Derrick seems to do everything, but it is cheerful and friendly, topped off by Derrick's impromptu calypso singing to entertain guests. Gluten-free and other diets can be accommodated.

$$$ La Cantina, Milford Rd, Crown Point, T6398242. Lunch, dinner and takeaway. A good place to come if you're in need of pizza. Generous sizes, tasty toppings, cooked in a wood-fired oven. Pasta also on the menu.

$$$ La Tartaruga, Buccoo Bay, by the pier from where glass-bottomed boats depart, T6390940, www.latartarugatobago.com. Mon-Sat 1830-2200. Italian restaurant café-bar, excellent Italian food, pizzas, pastas, reservations essential. Wine shop open from 1700.

$$$ The Seahorse Inn, across the road from the beach, next to **Grafton Beach Resort**, T6390686, www.seahorseinntobago.com. Daily 1200-1530, 1830-2200, happy hour 1730-1830 for drinks. Excellent dinners, beautifully presented, lots of seafood, lobster, shrimp and catch of the day. Good portions, yummy desserts, friendly service, extensive wine menu. Style is elegant rustic, sit upstairs overlooking garden and bar downstairs. Reservations essential. There are also 4 guest rooms if you want to stay.

$$$ Shirvan Watermill, on Shirvan Rd, T6390000. Daily 1700-2200. Specializes in seafood and steaks, elegantly presented, expensive and romantic, good service, fresh open feel.

$$$ Shore Things, 25 Old Milford Rd, Lambeau, T6351072, see facebook. Craft gift shop and café, great place for lunch with hummingbirds feeding outside and the chance of seeing turtles on the shore. The menu is eclectic but they are known for their carrot cake and coconut cream pie. Lunch specials on Fri need reservations.

🎵 Bars and clubs

Tobago *p84, maps p86 and p88*
Tobago is not as lively as Trinidad and, away from Crown Point, places tend to close before midnight at weekends and even earlier during the week. There are bars around the island where you can 'lime' with the locals and often there is live music at weekends, which might be drumming or pan, but generally nightlife is quiet. The larger hotels offer more frequent entertainment in high season but it is unlikely to set the world alight.

Azucar, 133 Shirvan Rd, T6310121. Tapas restaurant and bar with variable food and service but offering salsa lessons and salsa dancing every night from 2100.

Bago's Beach Bar, entrance to Pigeon Point. On the beach with sea grape trees for shade. Happy hour 1900-2000, karaoke on Sat, popular with the ex-pat crowd and visitors as a fairly upmarket rum shop for relaxing after a busy day on the beach.

Barcode, Scarborough waterfront, T6352633, www.barcodetobago.com, see facebook for events. Open 1800-0200. Lively sports bar in town with music events, karaoke on Thu, spacious outdoor deck, great setting. Fri lunch is **Sweet Hand Friday** when they serve local food: a meat dish with macaroni pie, peas and rice. At other times wraps, salads, chicken, juices and protein shakes are served. There are TV screens for sports events and a couple of pool tables.

Glasgow's Bar, Northside Rd, Parlatuvier. Spectacular setting high above the bay on 2 floors with a panoramic view. Alan Glasgow is a friendly and informative host and concocts a mean rum punch. A great pit stop on a tour of the island or for a sunset cocktail.

Green Shop (Pumpy's), opposite Milford Court, Canaan. Open any day, any time. An old-style rum shop popular with locals and visitors, whether for the after-work/before-dinner crowd or later drinkers. Bench seating, rum, ice and chasers.

Lyda's Rum Shop, Main Rd, Charlotteville. A traditional rum shop in a small wooden shack. Here you can lime with the locals in the shade, watching the world go by on the seafront, and set the world to rights.

Ocean View Bar, Pleasant Prospect, Shirvan Rd. Cliffside bar with great sea view from the al fresco bench seating under a roof, known for its Fri night lime when local food is served.

The Shade, Bon Accord Village, T2942811. Nightclub and place to party, beside **Green Palm Hotel**.

Sunday School on **Buccoo Beach**, is a big party starting at 2000 every Sun evening with live steel pan music, followed at about 2300 by a DJ playing until early in the morning, 0400. The music ranges from Jamaican Dancehall to R&B, taking in soca and hip hop, and is very loud. This is the main night-time activity on the island, a regular event and a great place to see Tobagonians let their hair down. Don't miss. However, do take precautions: go by taxi and arrange a time to be collected; take a small amount of cash and leave all valuables behind (rum and beer are cheap, as are the snack stalls and barbecue outlets); guard your pockets from theft; be prepared for sexual approaches even if you are already with your partner.

⊙ Entertainment

Tobago *p84, maps p86 and p88*
Casino Gambling/gaming at the **Crystal Palace Casino** in Scarborough, on the waterfront above Barcode, at the **Royalton** at Crown Point Hotel, and at **Sunset Palm Club**, Buccoo Junction, Mt Irvine.

Cinema Movietowne, Gulf View Mall, Lowlands, http://movietowne.com/. Open from 1300 and with late shows Fri, Sat.

O Shopping

Tobago *p84, maps p86 and p88*
Arts and crafts
Batiki Point, Buccoo Village, opposite beach facilities. Mon-Fri 1100-1800, Sun from 1800 during Sunday School. A cavern of colourful local and imported crafts. Owned by Tina Friman from Finland. Colourful wall hangings depicting local life, beautiful Indian sari/sarongs and jewellery. In-house designs for T-shirts and batiks.
Forro's Homemade Delicacies, The Andrew's Rectory, opposite the Fire Station, Bacolet St, Scarborough, T6392485. Local condiments, preserves and sauces are cooked and bottled in a cottage industry started by Eileen Forrester, wife of the Anglican Archdeacon of Trinidad and Tobago. Gift boxes of tropical fruit jellies, tamarind chutney and hot sauces are a wonderful souvenir of the island.
Shore Things, Lambeau. Mon-Sat 1000-1800. Locally produced artefacts. Giselle also offers light lunches with yummy desserts, sit and watch the birds and the view.

Food
Gourmet Foods at RT Morshead, off Shirvan Rd, Mt Pleasant, T6398855. Daily 0800-1800. More upmarket than **Penny Savers**, with imported and higher priced foodstuffs including cheeses and deli meats, wines and spirits.

Penny Savers Supermarket, at 3 locations: Canaan, T6398992, Carnbee, T6398816, and Scarborough, T6395549. Mon-Sat 0800-2000, Sun and holidays until 1300. This is the main supermarket and stocks a good range including pharmaceuticals. The Canaan store is the largest, has car park and ATM (blue machine).

Shopping centre
Gulf City Lowlands Shopping Mall, on the outskirts of Scarborough. Variety of shops and multiplex cinema.

O What to do

Tobago *p84, maps p86 and p88*
Birdwatching
Birdwatching is one of the most popular activities on Tobago. The island is home to about 210 species, and some 90 of these species breed here, including some not commonly seen on Trinidad. The national bird is the rufus-vented chachalaca, or cocrico, a type of noisy pheasant with a look of a turkey about it which makes quite a racket at dawn and dusk. There are 6 different hummingbirds, often attracted to feeders strategically placed on verandas, where they appear unaware of an audience. Blue-crowned motmots flit around spectacularly in the bushes, while the range of seabirds off Little Tobago is impressive, particularly Dec-Jul when the red-billed tropicbirds are breeding. Tobago is on a route for migrating birds, with those from South America arriving in May-Sep and those from North America in Nov-Mar, both

escaping winter in their latitudes. At least one birdwatching trip with a specialist guide is recommended. He will know where to find species you are interested in, will recognize their calls and be able to identify local and migrant birds. He is also likely to be something of a botanist and can tell you about the plants the birds live on and know where the fruiting trees are that they are feeding on. The best guides take only 2-3 people so you can move quietly and see more. This is more expensive, but you get what you pay for. There are several well-established birdwatching locations, including the Forest Reserve, Little Tobago and the sewage ponds near Pigeon Point, while the freshwater ponds around the Magdalena Grand Hotel are also rewarding, but there are also coastal ponds, mangroves and forest locations to explore. Don't forget your binoculars.

Darren Henry, T6394559, darren_tours@yahoo.com. A trained forester, Darren Henry now works as a tour guide, offering birdwatching and general nature tours. He is very knowledgeable on the symbiotic relationship between plants and birds as well as the medicinal uses for local plants.

Gladwin James, T6392231. Used by the Tropical Audubon Society and other birding groups, Gladwin is the son of Adolphus James, who for many years was the eminent guide in the field. He can call birds to him and knows where they all live and where their nests are.

Newton George, 3 Top Hill St, Speyside, T6605463, www.newton

george.com. The most experienced and authoritative guide on the island with an international reputation and encyclopaedic knowledge, he is also very friendly and fun to spend a day with. He and his wife, Dianne, have a hummingbird gallery at their home and all 6 hummingbirds come to the feeders. His day trip around Tobago includes wetlands and sewage ponds, Grafton Bird Sanctuary, VHL mangrove boardwalk and the adventure farm for hummingbirds. George also takes all-day trips to Trinidad, visiting the Asa Wright Centre during the day and the Caroni Swamp in the evening.

Peter Cox, T7515822, www.tobago naturetours.com. A naturalist, ecologist and specialist birdwatching guide, Peter Cox is an enthusiastic and knowledgeable all-rounder and can tell you as much about the geology of the island as the creatures that live on it, whether they are butterflies, lizards, iguanas, snakes, turtles or birds. He offers birdwatching, nature tours, sightseeing and turtle watching in season.

Diving

The waters around Tobago are known as an unspoilt diving destination and there are several reputable dive shops. Most species of hard and soft corals can be found, and there is a huge brain coral, believed to be one of the world's largest, off Little Tobago, which you can see on a glass-bottom boat tour. The parrot fish are nibbling away at it, but it is so large that they are not yet doing major damage. The Guyana current flows round the south and east shores of Tobago and supports a large variety of marine life. Dive sites are numerous and varied, with walls, caves, canyons, coral gardens and lots of fish. There is exciting drift diving but it is not recommended for novices. You are swept along the coral reef at up to 5 knots while, high above, manta rays flap lazily to remain stationary in the current as they sieve out the plankton. Manta rays are not as plentiful as they used to be, because of changes in the temperature of the current; they are best seen between Jan and Mar. Eagle rays and southern stingrays can also be seen. Some of the most popular sites are **Arnos Vale**, **Pirate's Bay**, **Store Bay**, **Man O'War Bay** and **Batteaux Bay**. In 1997 a new site was added, with the sinking of the *Scarlet Ibis*, renamed the *Maverick*, a 350-ft roll-on/roll-off ship. This artificial reef lies 100 ft deep on a sandy bed and coral has grown and schools of fish are living in the wreck. The deck has now collapsed but with care you can still swim through the hull. Another vessel was sunk in 100 ft of water off the point at Speyside in 2003. The aluminium hull is growing hard coral and creatures are now living there. **Snorkelling** is also excellent almost everywhere, with good visibility. **Association of Dive Operators in Tobago (ADOT)**, www.tobago scubadiving.com, keeps a list of member-operators who meet their safety standards. There is a hyperbaric chamber at the Roxborough Medical Clinic, T6394354, divingsuperintendent@yahoo.com.

Other dive operators who are not part of the ADOT but who are highly professional include:
Blue Waters Dive'n is at **Blue Waters Inn**, Speyside, T6605445, see facebook (**Blue Waters Inn** tends to be full throughout the year so book early.) This is a 5-star PADI facility, dives are around Little Tobago and all escorted by at least 2 dive masters because of the currents, although there are dives for all levels of experience. Full range of courses available.
Tobago Dive Experience, at **Manta Lodge**, T6604888, offers NAUI, BSAC and PADI certification, www.tobagodiveexperience.com.

Fishing

The offshore fishing season is Oct-Jun, with the peak time around Nov when wahoo are plentiful and Feb-May for blue marlin. Other fish caught are white marlin, swordfish, sailfish, tuna, barracuda and mahi mahi. In the area off the **Sisters Rocks** and **Giles Islands** in the north, the marlin can be too big to land with the equipment available although catches of over 600 lbs are regularly recorded. The island record was for a blue marlin weighing 1005.9 lbs caught during the annual **Tobago International Game Fishing Tournament** held in May 2013. Fishing charters are available at about US$500-600 for half a day and US$800-1200 for a full day for up to 8 people. Alternatively you can arrange to go out with a local fisherman in his pirogue if you have your own rods and equipment and are not bothered by the lack of navigation equipment, life vests, shade, refreshments etc. It will be less than a quarter of the price but he will expect to take home most of the catch after you've taken whatever you want to eat. It is also worth remembering that fishermen are not tourism professionals and you are going to be up to 8 hrs in their company out at sea in a small boat. Coastal and reef fishing are on offer all year round, mostly in the northwest between Crown Point and Plymouth where you can find tarpon. The best flats for bonefish are at **Friendship**, between the airport and Lowlands. Local men will fish on the Caribbean side of the island with a simple line while standing on a rock or jetty and in some villages you can still see seine fishing (pulling seine) when groups haul in the nets on to the sand. Help from visitors is welcome. There are several small boat operators who offer fishing among other attractions such as coastal tours, snorkelling and beach barbecues. You should conduct your own safety inspection and do not risk going out in bad weather. The following are the larger operators with a good safety record and excellent equipment.

Dillon's Fishing Charter, T6783195 (Capt Stanley), or T4945337 (Capt Santos), www.fishingtobago.com, have a 48-ft Viking Sport Fish boat, *Super Cool Too*.

Grand Slam Charters Tobago, T6831958 (Capt Kester), www.grand slamtobago.com. Offshore and inshore fishing and island cruises.

Hard Play Fishing Charters, T6397108 or T6823474 (Capt Gerard 'Frothy' De Silva), www.hardplay.net. Offshore and reef fishing and skiffs for flats fishing.

Golf
Mount Irvine Bay, T6398871. Green fee US$85 per day for 2 people with golf cart. The course is very pretty but in need of some serious maintenance as the greens are now full of clover. The clubhouse is run down but has some interesting photos of past golf masters, such as Tony Jacklin and others, who played here in the 1970s when it was in its heyday. Good for a holiday game but far off its previous standard.

Tobago Plantations, T6608800, www.magdalenagrand.com/activities/golf. Upgraded in 2013, the par-72, 18-hole championship course is the best on the island, built on a former coconut estate and now part of the Magdalena Grand Resort. There is a club house with pro shop and driving range and practice putting green. Green fees are US$72 for 18 holes if you are staying at the hotel and US$90 if you are not, with club rental US$62.50. There are lots of packages available if you plan to play or take lessons frequently.

Mountain biking
Tobago is criss-crossed with a network of trails through the mangroves and mountains, up steep hills, along ridges, over streams, past waterfalls and down to beaches to cool off. The scenery is stunning with views of bays and beaches around

the next corner, along shady, forested paths to the sound of birdsong, stopping to pick fruit for refreshment.
Mountain Biking Tobago, Orange Hill Rd, Prospect, T6399709, www.mountainbikingtobago.com. Prices range from US$40 per person for a 2- to 3-hr ride for beginner/intermediate riders to US$50 for a 3- to 4-hr ride for experienced bikers, with all equipment, snack and a guide.
Tobago Mountain Bike Tours, T3325872, www.tobagomountainbike.com. Tours cost US$45 per person for 3-4 hrs including all gear, refreshments and guide.

Sailing
Each year Tobago has a race week in May, sponsored by Angostura and *Yachting World* magazine; many crewing possibilities, lots of parties. The Regatta Village is in the grounds of the Crown Point Beach Hotel.

Although Trinidad is stuffed with marinas in Chaguaramas, Tobago is off the beaten track and the only services for yachts on the island are at **Store Bay Marine Services**, Unit 3, The Surf Shack, Pigeon Point Rd, Crown Point, T3905408, http://sbms.co.tt/ and on facebook. Their engineers can handle nearly all repairs and maintenance required and everyone is efficient and friendly, charging reasonable prices. They also provide laundry services, internet access and provisioning. There is no yacht charter business on Tobago; the waters around the island are hazardous. You can, however, rent dinghies, hobiecats, kitesurfers and windsurfers for use within Buccoo Reef where the waters are more sheltered.

Tour operators
Harris Jungle Tours, Golden Grove Rd, Canaan, T6390513/7590170, www.harris-jungle-tours.com. Harris Mc Donald offers hiking and birdwatching tours in the forest, with pick-up at 0530 so you can get there as the sun is rising and see the birds at dawn. It is also cooler then. An award-winning and certified tour guide, Harris is a lifeguard, tall, fit and capable. Tours are US$60-140, depending on numbers, and can include the forest, beaches, Little Tobago, Charlotteville, waterfalls and snorkelling. He also has his own guesthouse.
Simon McLetchie, T6390265, www.tobago-adventure.com. Taxi driver and tour guide offering a range of tours including birdwatching, Argyll waterfall, Little Tobago, Scarborough, coastal sightseeing and drop off and pick up for Sunday School.
Unique Tours Tobago, T3445431, www.uniquetourstobago.com and on facebook. Friendly and helpful Junior Thomas offers guided tours in his 4WD truck for sightseeing and birdwatching, boots and refreshments included.

Watersports
The larger hotels offer their guests hobie-cats, kayaks and other water toys, but for instruction and the best equipment it is best to contact the specialists.
Radical Sports Ltd, Pigeon Point Heritage Park, Crown Point, T6315150, www.radicalsportstobago.com. This

is the only windsurfing centre on the island. Windsurfing is best Dec-June but there can be strong winds later in the year. Professional instructors are available Dec-May and clinics are held in winter by professional coaches with Sportif International. Buccoo Reef protects the lagoon and the water can be flat calm with prevailing winds cross shore from the right. There is plenty of room for kitesurfing as well as windsurfing. You can learn to fly training kites on the beach before starting body dragging sessions in the water. Wakeboarding is also offered to allow you to get the feel of the board in the water at speed. Other watersports on offer include water-skiing, stand-up paddle boarding, kayaking and hobie-cat sailing, while they also have mountain bikes to rent. **Stand Up Paddle Tobago**, 54 Samaan Grove, Golden Grove Rd, Canaan, T6814741, www.standuppaddle tobago.com. Run by Duane Kenny, who offers a variety of tours and instruction on SUPs and kayaks, along the coast, in the swamps and mangroves, in the lagoon, at night to see the bioluminescence, or further afield to discover deserted beaches and waterfalls.

⊖ Transport

Tobago *p84, maps p86 and p88*
Air
See Getting to Trinidad and Tobago, pages 6-8, for details of the airport and how to get to Tobago by air.

Boat
See Transport, page 10, for details of boat services between Trinidad and Tobago.

Bus
Buses originate at Sangster's Hill in Scarborough (PTSC T6392293). One-way fares range from TT$2-8. The timetable can be found on www.ptsc.co.tt/tobago-depot. html. Every 45 mins to 1 hr 0500-2130, between **Scarborough** and **Crown Point** (airport), TT$2, 25 mins. **Scarborough–Plymouth** via Arnos Vale every 45 mins, TT$2. To **Charlotteville** every 3 hrs, 0430-2030 Mon-Fri, 0600-1930 Sat, 0900-1730 Sun, TT$8, 1½ hrs and then return. Also some maxis on this route.

   Route taxis and **maxi taxis** leave from Lower Scarborough for the west and from Windward Road for the rest of the island. The Crown Point Airport route is the best, every 15-30 mins, 0530-1830; Black Rock route is fair, every 30 mins Mon-Fri 0530-2030, every 60-75 mins Sat and Sun until 2000. Route taxis to **Charlotteville** start from Burnett Sq, the rate depends on whether the vehicle is minibus or car, 1-1½ hrs. Blue band maxi taxis run all over Tobago. They follow set routes but have no timetables, although they don't run after about 2100. Fares start from TT$3.

Car
The speed limit is 50 kph/30 mph on Tobago, although you'd never know it. Away from the southwest, however, you can sometimes not travel above

16 kph/10 mph because of all the potholes. There are dozens of car rental firms but not all of them enjoy a good reputation.

Alamo Car Rental, Crown Point, T6390644, www.alamo.com. **Carro Rentals**, Plymouth, T7843617, www. carrorentals.com. **KCNN**, T6822888, www.tobagocarhire.com. **Peter Gremli Car Rental**, Crown Point, T6398400. **Rattan's Car Rental**, rattanscarrental@yahoo.com. **Sheppy's**, Crown Point, T6391543, www.tobagocarrental.com. **Shermans Auto Rentals**, www.shermansrental. com. **Taylor's**, Castara, T3545743, www.taylorstobagoautorental.com. See page 12 for further details.

Cycle

Easy Goers Bicycle Rental, Milford Rd, Crown Point, T6818025, www.easy goersbikes.com. Mon-Sat 0900-1630, rents mountain bikes, road bikes, children's bikes, beach cruisers, unicycles and tandems. They also offer tours. See also Mountain biking, page 112.

Taxi

Taxi fares are clearly displayed as you leave the airport: to **Crown Point** US$6, **Pigeon Point** US$8, **Scarborough** US$11, **Mt Irvine** US$11, **Roxborough** US$28, **Speyside** US$50, **Charlotteville** US$65.

ⓘ Directory

Tobago *p84, maps p86 and p88*
Banks On Tobago, there are no banks in the north of the island. **ATMs** can be found at the airport, Penny Savers Supermarket on Milford Rd, in Charlotteville and in Scarborough. They accept Visa, Plus, MasterCard and Cirrus. **Medical services** There is a **hospital** in Scarborough, T6392551.

Contents

Footnotes

Index

Join us online...

Follow **@FootprintBooks** on Twitter, like **Footprint Books** on **Facebook** and talk travel with us! Ask us questions, speak to our authors, swap stories and be kept up-to-date with travel news, exclusive discounts and fantastic competitions.

Upload your travel pics to our **Flickr** site and inspire others on where to go next.

And don't forget to visit us at footprinttravelguides.com